"A warm and wise book. It will do much to strip away the superfluous terror and helplessness we feel in the presence of death."

—Sam Keen
Author of *Voices and Visions*

"An immensely rich book, full of wisdom."

—*Psychology Today*

"Every physician should read this book."

—Lee Sanella, M.D.

"Keleman's treatment of death and his affirmation of life inspires praise. Share this book with someone you love."

—Cultural Information Service

"An important book to be read by every philosopher."

—Peter Koesterbaum
Professor of Philosophy, California State College at San Jose

"In this simple and profound book Stanley Keleman has achieved the unimaginable: he has given us back dying as an integral part of our personal experiencing *and* he has made it an exciting and meaningful challenge."

—Maurice Friedman
Professor of Religious Studies, Philosophy,
and Comparative Literature, San Diego State University

". . . a great book—beautiful and potent."

—J. Samuel Bois, Ph.D.
Lecturer, University of California at Los Angeles

"*Living Your Dying* will be required reading for all my patients."

—Thomas A. Munson, M.D.

"*Living Your Dying* will enable us to understand what dying means and how it can give life a dimension previously unknown to us. More pertinently, it instructs us how we can die our own death rather than one programmed for us."

—Herman Feifel, Ph.D., Chief Psychologist
Outpatient Clinic, Veterans Administration

Living is movement, another word for it is process.
Living your dying is the story of the movement
of your life.

LIVING YOUR DYING

BY
STANLEY KELEMAN

A RANDOM HOUSE • BOOKWORKS BOOK

Copyright ⊃1974 by Stanley Keleman
All rights reserved under International and Pan American
Copyright Conventions.

First printing, November 1974 in cloth.
Second printing, December 1975, in paperback

Typeset by Vera Allen Composition Service, Castro Valley, California
    (Special thanks to Jody, Vera and Bob)
Printed and bound under the direction of Dean Ragland, Random House

This book is co-published by Random House Inc.
                             201 East 50th Street
                             New York, N.Y. 10022

                    and   The Bookworks
                            2043 Francisco Street
                            Berkeley, California 94709

Distributed in the United States by Random House, and simultaneously
published in Canada by Random House of Canada Limited, Toronto.

Library of Congress Cataloging in Publication Data

Keleman, Stanley.
    Living your dying.

    1. Death.   I. Title.   [DNLM: 1. Attitude to
death.   2. Death.   BD444 K29L 1974]
BD444.K39   128'.5   74-8154
ISBN 0-394-48787-7
ISBN 0-394-73166-2

Manufactured in the United States of America

for Gail, who gave me Leah,
a turning point in my life.

and to my friend and editor
Don Gerrard
without whose loving help and knowledge
there would be no book.

Books by Stanley Keleman

The Human Ground, Science and Behavior Books
Todtmoos, Lodestar Press
Your Body Is Alive and More, Simon and Schuster

Table of Contents

There is an old story that Plato, on his death-bed, was asked by a friend if he would summarize his great life's work, the Dialogues, in one statement. Plato, coming out of a reverie, looked at his friend and said "Practice dying."

Entering

This is a book about the experience of dying. But it's not written for the dying person. Instead it is intended for all of us who one day will die. It offers the opportunity to be more connected to your body and to experience how your body dies. It is about making the dying experience explicit.

What I am trying to say is that dying need not be fearful or painful, either socially or psychologically. Also that there may be no relationship between our *images* of dying and the *experience* of dying, between the *observation* of someone's death and the *feeling* of dying. The implication of these discoveries is that in this culture dying is an unknown phenomenon.

We live in a time that denies death, that distorts the dying experience by retaining traditional myths. What we need is a fresh start, a new myth, a new vision of maturity and longevity. We are not victims of dying; death does not victimize us. But we *are* victims of shallow, distorted attitudes toward dying, which we conceive as tragic.

A way to view dying can be based upon an understanding of the biological process — that our bodily life and our psychological life are the same. In twenty years' experience practicing therapy, working with people, sharing their lives, sharing where they have restrained themselves, how they have stopped their flow, witnessing how they try to free themselves, I have learned that the body pulsates like an ocean, that the life of the body is lived separate from social roles, and that inhibited grief restrains this pulsation and flow. I know that there is *a life of the body that is lived beside the social life and the personal life.* I believe that a new mythology for dying lies in this life.

Most people live their dying as they have lived their lives. People who rarely express themselves emotionally, or whose lives are lived as misery and defeat, tend to die that way. People whose lives are rich in self-expression tend to die self-expressively. But we do not have to die as we lived, as martyrs, cowards or heroes. We don't have to hide our deeper selves or our knowledge of who we wish we were.

Nature trains us to die by example and by experience. We witness dying on television, we read about it in the newspapers, we may see it in the streets. Everyone reacts differently to these experiences but our images of dying are formed here. It is reported that Goethe refused to hear of the death of his friends, and hid himself at the passing of funeral processions. He forbade the word death to be spoken in his presence and tried to cut death completely out from his existence.

When I talk about dying, it's on two levels. There's *big dying* and there's *little dying*. We are always losing and finding things, always breaking with the old and establishing the new. That's little dying. My experience, my myth, is that big dying is similar to little dying, at least in terms of process and of feeling. Our little dyings are meant to teach us what our big dying may be like.

Experiencing, the first section of the book, is about learning how to talk about what is evoked in us around little dyings. **Mythologizing,** the second section, is about replacing our social images of dying with our experience, thereby creating a new vision for our lives.

We are all more familiar with dying than we

suspect. Our bodies know about dying and at some point in our lives are irrefutably, absolutely and totally committed to it, with all the lived experience of the genetic code. The body knows how to die. We are born knowing about dying. It has been said that man suffered a shock when he discovered that dying, rather than being due entirely to accident or evil intentions, was a routine life event. One died. That shock is no less severe to us today. There are two major events in life. Birth is one. Dying is the other.

Many times when I ask people to tell me their fears of dying they say they have none. I ask whether they are worried about dying and they tell me no. When a person inhibits their feelings in this way it's called denial, or the ostrich syndrome. Persons who are connected to their denial of dying are just as much on the path of self-discovery as those who can directly experience their fears. Experiencing is the key to self-connection, self-formation and self-expression.

Dying and death are not synonymous; they are distinct and separate events. About death almost nothing can be known this side of parapsychology and faith. About dying a great deal can, since a pattern for dying is lived by *each person* in *their* lifetime. Living your dying is the body's living and dying. It is the shaping of the flesh.

Experiencing

Dying is about learning how to give up what we have embodied. Being alive is being incarnate, in the flesh. Dying is giving up form, is being embodied and being disembodied, being bounded and unbounded. We live in these two worlds. This section formulates a language to better understand our experience.

Styles of Dying

It's a pulsating world. Wherever I look, whatever I experience, under the microscope, through the telescope, with my bodily expressions, I see the phenomenon of *excitation*. Everything in motion is excited. There's a pattern of resonation, of harmonies. The living goes up and down, in and out.

Excitation, this fundamental characteristic of living, is a process that has two phases: *expansion* and *contraction*. As expansion, excitation is reaching out, expressive. Continued expansion is self-extending, leading beyond physical boundaries to the world of social interaction. As contraction, excitation gathers the self, becoming self-collecting and impressive, creating a more personal self.

I call these two characteristics *self-extending* and *self-collecting* They are fundamental to human life. Expanding from the biochemical environment to cellular activity, the life force organizes itself in systems and eventually in complex organisms. Enlarging and focusing on individuality, this excitement, expanding and contracting, becomes pulsation, seems to be characteristic of all life, is the alpha and omega of feeling and action. This activity, this organization of excitation, creates new life in the human child. Excitation increases after birth; it becomes self-expression when it establishes physical, psychological and social boundaries at the borders of the child's interaction with the world. As the child grows, these boundaries expand; excitation transcends self-expression, pushing past one's normal biological boundaries, connecting deeply within the world of social interaction. At this point, self-expression has become social expression, and new boundaries are formed. In this way, biological life and sociological life merge. Dying can occur anywhere in the continuum of this expansion as a natural stage in the development of excitation. Such dying is *eruptive*, or dispersive, the contained organism exploding, breaking out of its boundaries into the world. Strokes and heart attacks are common examples of eruptive dying. The event is usually sudden, and is one style of dying, one way the organism terminates itself.

The other way is its opposite. At some point

in the development of self-expression, excitation becomes self-inhibiting. The body is
capable of prohibiting a continued expansion of
itself. Think of the heart that fills with blood and
contracts, the stomach that fills with food and
contracts. The body gathers itself, collects itself,
withdraws from the social world. Here dying
occurs as a series of debilitating or self-
retreating events or as shock, a deep withdrawal,
moving toward complete inhibition. Such a
dying is most likely characterized by a series of
illnesses, often lengthy, each requiring a surrendering of parts of oneself. This style of dying I
call *congealing.*

In the congealing style, just as in the eruptive, there is still learning and experiencing,
revealing new perceptions and insights. The older, maturing persons need not conceive of
themselves as going downhill, but should see
themselves as being in a socially uncharted mode
of life.

There seem to be these two cycles in the
formative process — eruptive and congealing,
or expansive and solidifying. A person in the expansive phase disperses his experience into the
world. A person in the solidifying one gathers
his experience to himself. The thrust of

excitement, called life, expands and contracts, it pulses, eventually bursting its boundaries or shrinking into diminished boundaries. Dying in either style, either cycle, is not an interruption of life, but a continuation of it.

The lives of two famous men, Lyndon Johnson and Harry Truman, clearly show the self-extending and self-collecting characteristics that distinguished them. Lyndon Johnson lived and moved in a constantly expanding world of personal power — his political career accurately embodies my metaphor for the self-extending person. His influence seemed to be always growing. He began his career as a Texas schoolteacher and ended it as President, with world-wide influence. His death, from a heart attack, typifies dying in the eruptive style.

Harry Truman, a quiet man, moved from social beginnings as a Missouri store clerk, through a series of unusual political events to his position as President. But then his life changed, pulling in, pulling back, back to Missouri, shrinking social roles, no longer President, no longer politician, no longer money-maker, collecting himself, slowly diminishing his personal roles — lover, father, husband. His excitation, his life, was moving toward a simple organismic level, in which he continued to live but with diminished social or psychological impact upon the environment. Dying was a prolonged shrinking process. Truman's life is an example of dying in the congealing cycle.

Each of these styles has many variations. Each is a natural continuity of a general style of life expression. Self-extension reaches toward dying; self-collection withdraws toward it. Both styles are a direct expression of two sides of the pulsatory pattern of excitation, fundamental to the organism, fundamental to all life processes.

There are general patterns of biological activity observable in most everyone's life which reflect elements indicative of being in one dying cycle or another. For example, some people seem to have trouble getting to bed and others have trouble getting out of it. Some people have trouble falling asleep at night. Others have trouble waking up in the morning. The first group I call self-extenders, always moving out into the social world. They seem to gain experience best from interacting with other people. The second group, the self-collectors, seem always to have more contact with themselves than with the world. They seem to prefer privacy. They want to experience themselves deeply and usually alone. These people are not as likely to be foreigners to changed experiences as the self-extenders. They may see affirmation in this book while self-extenders see new territory.

The myths of all societies try to ensure that we do not die meaningless deaths. They try to give an avenue of approach to the dying process so that we are not swept away in despair at meaninglessness. For those who find it meaningful, they offer a social way of dying. And for those who cannot or do not have an inkling of the possibility of their own way of dying, a way. In this manner myth tries to provide for each individual to participate in his termination.

Death and dying for us are hidden behind out of date attitudes that romanticize the process. They are a subtle form of denial. Some of these mythologies and their styles of dying are:

The hero's death. Enveloped in images of violence, the person dies bravely, nobly. Death is an enemy to fight. At the last it's better to take your own life than be victimized by death. A flamboyant death.

The wise man's death. This is the death of resignation. There is nothing anyone can do about death, it is inevitable, so accept it. Death is a sleep, a blessing, a return to nature, or the end of one's earthly task. A submissive death.

The fool's death. I am not really dying. Death is a kind of cosmic joke; I shall come back. There is no death anyway, just rebirth. This is the senseless, aimless death.

The martyr's death. To give your life is noble; sacrifice for love or for a social cause, or to express life's stupidity. I will permit myself to be killed. My death will be important to society. The victimized death.

The morbid death. Death is a grim reaper; his approach is terrifying, fearful, painfully unholy. Death is an executioner, man is the victim, avoidance and denial the only remedies. A bizarre dying.

Each of us lives our variations on these mythologies of dying which are expressed at turning points in our lives overtly or implicitly.

There is currently a lack of mythology for the death of the body. There is no place for its life either. In present mythology, the body is treated as a tool, a slave, an instrument, an endentured servant, a suit of clothes, a something to be overcome. The body is forced to live the life the mind wants to live, and to die for the mind's ideals. It is no wonder that there is fear and terror at facing one's last days. The mind is terror-stricken, not only because it fears facing the void of extinction, but also because its source is about to abandon it. The body that has fed, housed and transported the mind prepares to depart, and the mind wants to survive the body's dying.

We are living witnesses, through our lives and the lives of family and friends, of how the mind faces or avoids dying. We witness as bodies the living out of our mythologies. And what is our witness; what do we experience? Unintegrated lives, unlived lives, partially fulfilled lives, unlived bodies, stressed bodies, worn-out bodies, premature aging, guilt, anger, fear and denial.

Our negative social attitudes toward the body and toward its right to a wholesome life deny us the right to die in our own way. In living the life of the society we don't realize we also die its death.

I remember when my grandfather suffered a massive stroke at home the doctor ordered him to the hospital, where he died soon after. My grandmother was full of anger and guilt for not having let him die at home, surrounded by the family, feeling comfortable, guided and guarded in his last hours, instead of dying in the land of strangers. He did not die his Jewish death. When she died, my grandmother did not die in the hospital, but at the home of my aunt. She had learned how she wanted to die.

The basic metaphors in my work are taken from the language and images of the body. Experiencing yourself as bodily, you experience body and mind as one — a living person, a somebody. The body metaphor allows the development of a new attitude toward living and toward dying. I have developed this metaphor more fully in *My Body Is Alive and More.**

We live our lives, our dying, consciously and unconsciously, voluntarily and involuntarily. We participate in our life or deny it. And we can, to some extent, reconstruct our life in our awareness, experience it anew and make changes in it. That, too, is what this book is about. Read what Rilke the poet had to say about dying in 1910.

"The desire for a death of one's own is growing more and more rare. In a little while it will be as rare as a life of one's own. Heavens! it is all there. We come and find a life ready for us; we have only to put it on. We go when we wish or when we are compelled to. Above all, no effort. Voilà votre mort, monsieur. We die as best we can; we die the death that belongs to the disease

*Simon & Schuster, 1975.

from which we suffer . . . In sanatoria, where people die so willingly and with so much gratitude to doctors and nurses, they die from one of the deaths assigned to the institution; that is regarded very favorably."*

The Notebook of Malte Laurids Brigge, Rainer Maria Rilke, trans. John Linton, The Hogarth Press, London 1959.

Turning Points

Important events occur in everyone's life that are the focus of new directions. These turning points signal that one way of living is over and a new way is emerging; they are rites of passage in the life. They are turning points. Think of the first day at school; the beginning of adolescence; the first job; the first sexual encounter; the funeral of a parent; the birth of a child; the onset of menstruation.

Turning points are emotional journeys. They are life's upswellings. They are the intersections and intensifications of new encounters, new images, new impulses, catalyzing, brewing riches, charging the atmosphere. They are the roots of new directions and self-formation. They are the shapers of our bodies.

A screaming "I don't want to die like this!" awoke me from my sleep. It was my father. His pain was excrutiating, for him, for me, for my family. My father's sicknesses were always accompanied by his fear — that he might die in pain. I, we, would be, were helpless, would be left helpless. Fear, resentment, helplessness, guilt, sadness, confusion. Die like what? In pain? Before his time? Unlived.

I had wondered about old people dying, or about murders, but this was my first serious encounter with dying. And it was repeated in many ways in the next few years.

This experience was a major event, a turning point, a step in my life that galvanized me out of my childhood into the beginning of my manhood. I had just become bigger, older, wiser. The fragility of me, of those around me, and of our finiteness was born. I knew something. I thought differently. I felt differently. I had to realign myself to the world I knew, for it was no more. I became serious. A bit of melancholy stepped into my life.

Years later, my father had a heart attack. I was there at his side. He asked me to hold his hand. This was another turning point for me. I grasped instantly his silent, pleading "I don't want to die like this!" I understood my father had not lived his life, that he was sick and dying as an expression of his unlived possibilities, of his helplessness, and as a statement of trying to change his life.

Discovering our dying is a turning point. Dying is like the first day at school. Dying evokes helplessness, the unexpected, challenging the known. Dying establishes new directions, gaining new powers, losing the old. Giving up action patterns, thought patterns, being unsure, being excited, knowing something is emerging but not knowing where it's going. Dying, like any turning point, is a place of transition, a facing of the unknown and the emerging complexity of new ways of being. New actions, thoughts, feelings. Each turning point is the resolution of loss and an encounter with the unknown. The unknown consists of that which we do not recognize or find unpredictable and of our feeling helpless in the face of it.

With each new turning point we tend to repeat and expand on the manner in which we handled previous ones. What is learned in the first day at school, for example, lays a base for social patterns which is repeated and strengthened by our succeeding turning points. In this way patterns of action or non-action, of thought and fantasy, of feelings expressed or withheld become repeated, regularized and fixed. In this way each person becomes who he knows himself to be. Each person becomes comfortable with his response to change or to crisis — with his fears, unevoked feelings, body movements, tensions, little withdrawals.

These patterns do not develop at random. They are built on each individual's inter-pretation of and responses to prevailing social myths. The two most dominant myths in our cul-ture are modeled around sexual roles. Most males develop patterns around the heroic myth — images of strength, of conflict, of strug-gling against something threatening or evil. St. George slays the dragon. The male is tough, ag-gressive, never shows his feelings, carries on the family lineage and is willing to die (bravely, without complaint) for his cause. The female is expected to develop patterns around the martyr myth — images of service and sacrifice, giving her life to help her mate and children achieve their goals, always supporting others, easily ex-pressing feelings of love and feelings of loss, permitting her will to be killed for this cause, waiting always to be rescued by a male, always being the victor's prize.

Such patterns are learned first in the pre-school years. Little boys play soldiers; little girls play with dolls. As one grows older, variations develop. The successful or wealthy person lives the wise man's myth. Life is as it should be. Death is a sleep. A resignation. Accept it. The un-successful or frustrated person lives the fool's myth or the morbid, defeated myth. Life is an evil joke, a trap. Reject it, defy it. Dying is meaningless; death is the ultimate insult.

Each person lives his turning points. Each person handles them uniquely. Upon popular social myths, personal myths and personal fantasies are laid. Myth provides a structure for each person's life at these subtle levels, unobstrusively, a structure for the expression of human energy through actions, thought, feelings, sensations and body attitudes. And turning points evoke expressions of anger, pain, excitement, loss, sacrifice, grief and others. Becoming aware of how you handle turning points is experiencing yourself, is discovering how you live with little dying. Living your dying is learning about the transformation arising from your turning points.

This diagram is the formative loop that I draw to represent the excitation around turning points. It represents how boundaries are surrendered and how boundaries are formed.

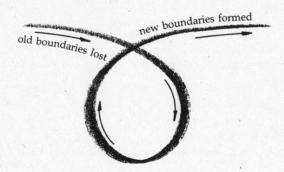

The descending side of the loop is where loss occurs, where new space is created and where the emotional reactions to loss and to space are experienced. The ascending side is where new excitement is sensed, where new possibilites are organized, where new boundaries are formed. In the descending side old thoughts, ideas, feelings, action patterns and connectedness are given up. In the ascending side new thoughts, intuitions and feelings are transformed into action patterns and new connections are made. This cycle is the energetic process from which the styles of dying and feelings are formed in action patterns as new connections are made.

Life can be described as a migration through many formative loops, many little dyings. Growth, change and maturing occur by deforming the old and forming the new. In these little dyings we can learn how to live our big dying.

Turning points are the cauldron of our lives, the steps of our birthings, our self-formings. There are no turning points that are not accompanied by feelings of dying; no self-forming occurs without endings and loss.

Excitement: To Be Roused, To Be Wakened

Excitement is the glue that binds us to the world. When loss occurs, excitement is unbounded. This loss of connection produces disorientation and fear, but it also provides the energy necessary to the forming of new relationships. Dying generates excitement, unformedness, unconnectedness, unknowingness.

There is a curiosity about dying — part is wanting to know; part is dread — being afraid to know. We can't admit we want to know; we're not supposed to admit it. We live in a state of ambivalence, a mixture of pleasure and fear. There is the fear of the unknown and there is the fear of knowing.

Excitement is the force that connects sex and dying — this is sensed by all of us. Every act of sex is like an act of dying — its converse should also, could also, be true. How excitement is handled, how excitement expresses itself, surging and ebbing, is the mystery of life. Sex we say is pleasurable; dying we say is fearful. But both are life expressions — expansive, reaching out, transcending boundaries, going beyond ourselves, changing ourselves, entering the unknown, being unknown. Or shrinking, pulling away from, making separations, going to the depths of our personal cosmos.

Excessive preoccupation with violence has a close relationship to sexuality. Pictures of killing are male orgastic images in which the body is broken into, opened to the world, in which something comes out, something appears, something changes, the gun points at you and the big explosion occurs. Notice that we don't have female sexual images of dying. To me all violent images are orgastic; they're the excitement that erupts into the world. The are full of all the symbols of sex, of course; but besides those, and more importantly, they are full of the excitement that knows unity, the longing to merge that is basic to life.

People who believe that dying is only morbid, pitiful, sad or tragic see only the public images. There are those people who face dying in high risk professions, who risk dying even though it is frightening, who love to live in this constantly intensified state. The mystery of dying is not full of fear for everyone. Not everyone rages against the darkness, or meekly submits to it.

Sexual activity has two sides to it, flavors of attaction and flavors of repulsion, flavors of hard and of soft, love and aggression, personal and impersonal. There is this same hide and seek with dying. Does not denial heighten feeling and curiosity? Is there a person alive who isn't deeply curious about what dying will be for them? Is there a person alive who would not like their dying full of excitement?

Wilhelm Reich pointed out that the culmination of sexual excitement peaking in orgasm is a way of getting out of ourselves into the universe. Orgasm takes us from the world of the known into the world of the unknown, experiencing our unboundedness for a brief time, giving us a hint of what our dying may be. When we have orgastic experiences, we are saying "I let go, I give, I risk, I die, I melt, I become one, I go to the cosmos, I surrender for a few minutes to the unknown." People can be afraid to say "I love you" and "I wish I could die" in the same breath. Or, "I feel this love as a melting into the universe, like dying," or "I'm surrendering all my life outward now." People have learned not to say that, not to feel that.

A woman said to me that her greatest wish, when she is having an orgasm and feels herself beginning to melt away, is that she could just keep going. She told me she wants to melt into the cosmos and not come back. There are many ways to be in the world. There are many ways to leave it.

Emotion: To Migrate, To Move Out

We are always living with feelings of loss, feelings of helplessness, feelings of pain, feelings of anger and feelings of fear that emerge around turning points. Whenever we are unbounded, whenever excitement is free, feelings surge. Some of them plague us, terrorize us in the night.

The unexpected froze me when I was told my friend was dead. Dead. On that nice day! The shock of disbelief choked off my crying, but I felt I should cry. I should show sadness, hurt, but my disbelief, anger, erupted first. I shouted "What do you mean? What happened?" I blamed myself, others, I blamed her. The next day I compulsively, relentlessly had to find out what happened, every detail of her dying. Senselessness, utter senselessness was my pain. Why should this have happened at age thirty-seven? The blaming anger muted my sadness, trying to fill the hole I felt in my life.

At the funeral, when the others left, I wept deeper than I have ever wept in my life. I wept out the unsaid and the unlived. And the wrench of separation became real. The sadness filled me and diminished the feeling of being cheated, of being alone, of having the dying take place unexpectedly, without me. All I had was an imagined ending. From alive and vital to nothing. Now a hole. I went home with my memories, my feelings, a different dialogue.

This turning point altered my life and my feelings, deepening my knowledge about the price of holding back, of softening one's commitment. From the torrent of my feelings and confusion around her death arose the beginning of excitement that allowed me new relationships I took into my present life what I had shared with her in my past, and more.

I found that mourning could be expressed in crying, in singing, in moaning, in catharsis, or in withdrawal, retreat, isolation, contemplation, prayer. Sometimes my feelings occurred eruptively, sometimes congealingly. I cried out in pain, or stiffened up. Pain carried me outside myself or shrunk me into a ball.

Letting go is the willingness to experience unconditionally but that may be possible only when someone dies. Letting go means violating

the rule never to give in to the body. Letting go mobilizes feelings of helplessness. We are "at a loss" to know what to do. The pain of loss intensifies this helplessness.

Paradoxically, not all loss mobilizes these feelings. Some losses we identify as good riddance, and we thank our lucky stars for them. Look how some people blossom when their spouses die.

In all my years of doing therapy the fear of being lonely emerges as one of the most consistent fears people have. This fear is strong enough that it prevents people from ending negative relationships. To many people a negative or destructive relationship is preferable to being lonely. There are people who will make all kinds of sacrifices in order not to risk the feeling of their emptiness. Other people express this fear as a feeling of being overwhelmed with sensations.

Fear and anger are the basic defense reactions in life. Fear is a self-collecting response, anger a self-extending one. Fear and anger — retreat and attack. One uses either of these reactions to try to hold their boundaries together and to prevent change or loss.

My world is fragmented suddenly by someone's dying. I may feel angry that they are leaving me, or afraid that I'll be left alone. My response is an attempt to fill in the empty spaces or to act as a bridge to a new space. When Alan Watts died suddenly toward the end of 1973, my first reaction was anger. "My God, why did you go and do such a thing at this time!" Watts had let me down by not living up to my expectations of him. I needed him, but he was gone.

Anger and fear, expansion and contraction, are perfectly natural responses even though they don't always fit the expected social image of sadness or grief at someone's dying. But more important, they are responses necessary to the person, responses that act to preserve the person's integrity, their wholeness, and to avoid or correct the broken boundary.

Just as I may both love and hate someone, so part of me may want someone to die and part of me does not. Part of me is understanding and part resentful as all hell. Part of me grieves when someone else dies and part of me might realize that their dying has given me a gift. That somehow that person's dying makes me freer or emptier or challenges me with new possibilities.

Anger is a powerful emotion for resolving one's ending. A woman I knew was dying of cancer. She told me about seeing her deceased husband asking for help in a dream. She refused him angrily. Her daughter was surprised at her unrelenting anger and at her denial of the husband. The woman's answer was that in this way she could, for the first time, express her resentment about her lifelong martyrdom. She died her protest; she did not relent.

Helplessness is the basic pain of life. A wound that triggers what we recognize as pain — which is a disturbance in the body's integrity — sends a message "do something". The stronger the disturbance, the stronger the message. When we cannot do for ourselves, when we cannot respond to relieve the pain, that state pushes all the survivial buttons. Even a child is not so helpless. To the degree that we find ourselves unable to respond to ourselves, pain escalates and overwhelms or threatens to overwhelm us. The most real pain is our help-lessness.

Nina Bull* told me an interesting story about her discovery of the relationship between awareness and pain. On going to the dentist, she realized that she tried to prevent pain by tight-ening up. All she really did was localize the pain in her mouth and deaden herself all over. In fact, pain thus localized became more acute. And the price she paid for localizing the pain was that she

*Author of: *The Attitude Theory of Emotion; The Body and Its Mind*

had to diminish or disassociate the rest of herself. I think we all make this mistake in trying to
deal with our pain.

Nina's story taught me that tightening up,
contracting, localizing what's happening to us
can be self-defeating. Her story made me think
of Sigmund Freud's very penetrating observation that in our psychological life every denial
is an affirmation.

Sacrifices

Sacrifices are silent bodily expressions of turning points. They are bargains or pacts by which we seem to try to gain the right to live, or to make our lives too valuable to take away. They are bargains struck between several different parts of ourselves, or with others, that call for the curtailing or surrendering of some of the self. Sacrifices are the deals we make in crisis situations, forcing a commitment to our own self-inhibition. But there's more than survival implied in a sacrifice. In effect we are forming ourselves in our bargaining. Without sacrifices we can never become somebody. Sacrifice is a characteristic of everyone's formative process.

Every sacrifice has two parts. In exchange for the modification or blocking out of our fears we agree to live part of somebody else's life style, and embody that attitude in our musculature. The bargain is between the roles we can and cannot live, between the feelings or thoughts we can or cannot allow to exist. The decision is to embody ourselves in a specific way, for which we agree to do something. "As long as I'm not going to die, I'll be such and such a kind of person." "I'll be a good boy so don't threaten to hurt me," which could be translated "Don't threaten to kill me, or don't threaten to ostracize me." The sacrifice could read "I'll do what you want if you don't reject me." Then the doing of what they want gets embodied as a muscular contraction, which you call your chronic stiff neck or a pet belief. The bargain that is made is reflected in how you choose not to act.

The sacrifice involves a promise not to fail and a promise to live up to someone else's goals — a mother's, a family's, a culture's. This implicit concept of the denial of failure is an intimate part of the bargain. You promise, no matter what, not to lose control, not to betray your part of the deal. This leads to a most powerful fear of dying, which springs from the secret knowledge that by keeping the bargain we have not lived our real desires.

Making a sacrifice also means projecting ourselves into some future time. "I won't live my present impulses now." "I won't be too sexual now, only when I'm married." "I won't really do what I want to now. I'll do it after I fulfill my ambition." This is the part that must be limited or unfulfilled.

In our earliest years, we make our bargains with the other world — the world outside ourselves — usually with our parents. "I won't have a tantrum," "I won't cry," "I won't make you anxious," "I promise to listen" — things like that.

When children first begin going to school, they have to learn to give up parts of themselves in order to gain acceptance or approval. They may have to surrender or inhibit being spontaneous in order to win the teacher's approval. They may have to postpone gratifications. They may have to do without their mothers. They may have to sacrifice a world in which they were the center of attention in order to be part of their new group. How the child learns to do these things, what they have to give up, what they have to stop doing, is the sacrifice.

Later, the bargain comes entirely from within. We promise ourselves we'll do good deeds, we promise ourselves we will not do what hurts other people, we make ourselves do unto others as we would have them do unto us. We begin to make a whole series of bargains with ourselves about our conduct in the social world.

The classic sacrifice is expressed "If I am a good boy or a good girl, something I fear won't happen to me." Variations can go like this: "If I am a charitable person, poverty won't happen to me." "If I am a good mother, I will live longer." "If I am a wise and generous leader, I will not be killed." "If the teacher likes me, the thing I fear won't happen." "If I work hard, Daddy will love me and I won't be abandoned." This behavior attempts to ward off whatever situations, images or feelings a person believes creates the possibility of their dying, softening dying a little for them.

Betraying our sacrifice suddenly confronts us with specters of guilt and punishment, or of the unknown, which is part of our fear. To challenge a sacrifice is to face the same emotional forces which drove us to make it in the first place. This dilemma creates a new reality for us, one in which the sacrifice itself becomes a defense against feelings or images of dying and their consequences.

To betray a sacrifice is to place ourselves under the threat of being helpless, and of our ideas and feelings of what dying will be like. In any dangerous situation our reaction mechanism tries to stop the danger or eliminate it. The brain calls for a muscular action, a contraction. That chronic muscular contraction apparently wards off, distances us from dying or slows and encapsulates our life processes. Our perception is "I have saved myself."

I perceive myself under the threat of death. I am panicky. Then I perceive that with a muscular contraction I have altered myself and saved myself. I have fantasized an alternative. "I can't go forward; I gotta go back." "I can't do it that way; I'll do it like this." "I can't get along with this person; I've got to find another one." Whatever the alternative we work out, it comes from the imaginative life. The price of this feeling of self-preservation is a diminution of our being and the acceptance of a fantasized existence, such as "In this way I will live longer." Chronic contraction inhibits us moving into the world.

Here is the connection between psychic danger and living a fantasized alternative to what evokes the danger as a basic life attitude. In learning what to avoid and how, we create action patterns, the consequences of which are perceived as real limitations and as real freedoms. "I cannot live out who I really am." The lived fantasy is deeply associated with the feeling of dying which has created it. Our social world is created on the basis of this kind of contradiction, a part of which we carry around inside us all our lives.

I first experienced some of my sacrifices by trying to learn how they expressed themselves through my gestures, my thoughts and my feelings. Who is this character I have become? What are the roles that I play in life that I call me? What muscular contractions shape me into these roles like a suit of clothes I cannot take off? How have I learned to smile all the time, or frown, or be so forceful or timid? These attitudes are a part of the language of the body and of how I use myself socially.

Grief and Mourning

Grief and mourning have to do with being abandoned and with loss. They are the natural consequences of the loss of boundaries. All grief and mourning is about severed connectedness, which gets translated in how we do or don't make endings. Grief is the feeling of loss at the interrupted or broken connection, and mourning is the process of incorporating that loss into our lives. Grief usually begins with the unexpected, and is the emotional expression of this newly-created space or ended connection. Mourning is the process of working through that grief.

There are many similarities between grief over someone else's dying and grief over your own, or between mourning the loss of a friend and mourning the loss of yourself. They may be the same. In both cases your mourning process generally follows the same pattern: initial shock; the welling-up of feeling and emotional expression; working through unendedness; reaching new relationships with yourself and others.

In both cases the object of your grief and mourning is yourself, but in one case you are the sur-
vivor and in the other you are not. A person may
be able to learn from his grief and mourning experiences with people how to grieve and mourn
the loss of himself.

It is almost always true that with the emotional impact of someone's death or imminent
death we feel that their dying is tragic. We have
an image that the person's death is an interruption of their life, is not how that person's life
was supposed to be. However, tragic and fearful
feelings are not a universal response. It is not the
only way to view someone's death. It is, in fact, a
peculiar cultural notion, an idea most likely to
occur to an impersonal observer, someone
removed from the succession of organismic
events through which the dying person has
lived. This concept — that someone's death
need not be an unhappy event, or tragic, or an interruption to their organismic existence, but the
logical termination of their process — gives a
wholly different feeling for and image of
another's death, and of your own death. A person's death may be perceived as socially tragic in
that they died before fulfilling an obvious or expected destiny (John F. Kennedy is a good example). But of course the organism does not give social realities the highest priority. The reverse

situation also occurs, because mourning doesn't have to mean sadness and loss. Someone's death may be perceived as a relief, or even as a joy, a new freedom. I think of the reports of ecstasy over the news of Stalin's death. In fact, the same person's death may trigger many different responses, from grief to joy. But for every person involved, no matter their particular emotion, there is a mourning.

Mourning is the freedom to express feelings that weren't or couldn't be expressed under normal life circumstances. Mourning the death of others is a way to rehearse our dying. But mourning is not only this. It is also a ritual for the expression of some of the deepest and most intimate feelings of our existence.

If you inhibit the outwardness of your grief, you may get sick. You may begin to mourn with chronic depression, or engage in anxious behavior, or repetitive ritualistic behavior (such as tics or continual handwashing) or excessive, uncontrollable anger. Unlived grief can cause pain, depression, fear and bizarre behavior, like continuing a dialogue with the deceased in fantasy as if they were still alive, trying to maintain the old relationships, not deferring to the necessity for a new one. Each of us is afraid to express anger and sadness, afraid to cry and mourn the

loss of parts of ourselves that we have had to surrender at different stages of our lives. Each of us
is afraid to lose control of ourselves in this way.
But when grief cannot be properly expressed, it
will emerge as part of our unlived lives — our
fantasies and our fears.

A young woman I met dramatically released
the emotions she had lived with since the death
of her father. The event was a workshop on dying
and death. The woman arrived along with twenty
or more other people. The group went around
the circle, everyone introducing themselves, until it came to this woman, who seemed almost
unable to speak. She was an attractive person in
her early twenties, and she was deeply upset. She
held her head to one side and seemed to have difficulty speaking. As soon as she had told us her
name she blurted out that her father had died of
cancer just two weeks previously. Off and on
over the two days of the workshop, her whole story came out.

She was upset because she had no feelings
for her boyfriend, and she was upset because her
father had died. She felt very angry that her father seemed to submit so meekly to his fate at the
hands of the doctors, and that he had left her. She
felt jealousy toward her mother, who she felt
didn't really love or appreciate the martyred fa-

ther. She wanted her father's love and felt angry and frustrated that she had lost him both to her mother and to death. At the funeral she had secretly placed a rose in his coffin.

The point I want to make is two-fold. First, the complexity of feelings this woman expressed toward her parent and herself is common to everyone, but frequently kept hidden because of fear and shame. Second, as she expressed her feelings over the course of the workshop, this woman visibly reduced her anxieties and her tensions, at times recovering her natural voice. I do not know whether she was under professional care and I never saw her again, but this part of her life clearly demonstrates a dilemma common to many people. Grief that is not expressed emerges as disturbed behavior, organic or social.

A part of this woman's experience, and of everyone's experience, is that there is no socialization of mourning. Most people do not talk with anyone about dying — theirs or anothers — because no one plays the necessary role that makes such talk convenient. Few priests, doctors or funeral directors want to get involved with the emotional processes of dying. But you cannot deny people's experiences. Everyone has images of aging, isolation, sickness, pain, dying, the hereafter. Usually one holds these images and their corresponding fears inside until they get triggered by grief and by loss.

How we talk about mourning another person's dying relates to our own death. How we react to another person's death is how we will react to our own. Each of us in our lifetime mourns the loss of friends and of stages of our existence such as childhood and adolescence. These experiences can instruct us in our mourning process. Through them we can learn how to mourn ourselves and how to grieve for ourselves.

Part of the self-mourning process is that we grieve the death of our bodies, and of our social selves. We grieve for the loss of the depth of the relationships that our bodies were able to maintain, and that our social selves were able to maintain. We absolutely have to deal with that. The death of the body is the death of the body and we have to mourn it. I see in the death of others my own death. I sit by the deathbed of another and hold their hand, but I meditate upon my own dying.

I remember that, some years ago, when a girl friend of mine died, I mourned her for quite a while. And my mourning swung from deep sadness to anger. I felt that her death was unjustified (she died in an accident) and I was angry at her stupidity for killing herself. My emotions were deep sadness, crying, longing, and anger. One day she came to me in a dream. She said to me that my difficulty was that I was trying to prevent the inevitable. Then I understood that part of my grieving was caused by my not accepting that fact. Everyone's dying is inevitable. I just kept rehearsing over and over again all the things that could have been done to keep her alive and all the things she could have done. And so in the dream she reminded me that I was trying to do the impossible. That dream was a humbling experience for my ego. But I still raged. Then I had another dream, and this time my girl friend said, "Why don't you let me go? You're torturing me by holding on to me." Later I could have explained this dream as similar to somebody alive coming to me and saying "You're torturing me by holding on to me with all those negative feelings, or all those loving feelings." I understood the mourning was over and I had to let go of her image. And she was gone. That now there was a new relationship, she was part of me and she was also gone. And in this way I had finally ended my mourning.

Endings

Turning points are the ending of the old and the beginning of the new. They evoke how we end events. How we prohibit or participate in endings. We fear endings, desiring to leave events unevoked.

There are several ways endings occur. Think of a broken egg, spilling out from its boundaries. Or there is the hard-boiled egg, solidifying or rigidifying, that encapsulates itself like a ball in space that has no connection with the world. We may experience our space as empty or dense, unfilled or overfilled.

Endings bring us face to face with the unknown. Endings force us to make new relationships, or at least offer that opportunity. Mourning is the consequence of leave-taking and of endings. Endings may be said to be the cornucopia of a turning point. Many people will say "That person is irreplaceable to me." The truth of the matter is that making an ending forces us to start being more self-reliant, or at least offers that opportunity.

But people avoid endings. The feelings are too permanent. Endings and endedness scare people. Instead there is flight, withdrawal and rationalization. Keep the dead person's room intact. Act as if nothing has changed. All the clothing, all the pictures, all the personal items remain in place as though ready for use. Keep our feelings at the same even level. Avoid loneliness. This is an unending. Become stoic, realistic. Or the dead person never existed and any space they occupied is denied. A sharp finiteness. The first situation extends the past into forever; the second severs the connection forever. In either case nothing unexpected happens. That includes all those things we feel guilty about, wish we could change, wish had never happened, that make us feel uncomfortable, ashamed, resentful, afraid, sad — all the disappointments that represent all the unrealized potentialities for better contact or emotional completeness.

Unended events must get ended before we can let the dead person or the dead self die. This is true even when it's about a person physically dead many years. We carry that person around inside us, unable to part with them, unwilling to

accept the empty space, unwilling to complete a cycle. It is as though we could prolong our own life, or the life of another person, by refusing to change the emotional relationship.

Endingness is an important part of the mourning process. Working through our endings allows us to redefine our relationships, to surrender what is dead and to accept what is alive, and to be in the world more fully to face the new situation. Just as mourning is a time of emotional freedom, endings present the possibilities for expressing that freedom.

Unendedness comes up when we talk about our relationships to parents or friends from whom we are separated by distance of death and all the things we wanted to say or do, or didn't want to say or do. For instance: "I can't say good-bye to my father. I always wanted to tell him 'I hate your guts," or "I always wanted him to know I understood his dilemma." Unendedness includes aborted expressions, in which the consequences of expression are not followed up — like "I hate you" left hanging because the connection is broken.

We resist leave-taking because it seems so much like being abandoned. Intimacy has such a low priority for us that at the end of life we have been intimate with only a handful of people.

Everyone practices a mutually-agreeable non-verbal pact to keep a certain distance. When that line is crossed, feelings of anxiety come out. We feel we are about to lose control, or power.

Parting, ending, seems like a similar loss of orientation, or of control. We see ourselves a small speck in a limitless universe. Intimacy can be used as a safe harbor. Saying good-bye — losing an intimacy — evokes the same response of disorientation as an invasion of intimacy from without. We are afraid to cut loose, to drift through the infinite space, to drift through the society, to lose connection, to float in the social cosmos. The fear is a loss of contact. We fear we won't be able to be intimate in a new situation.

Ending reinforces the image that life is a finite, linear connection, and that to break the connection, to lose the contact, is to lose the life. With leave-taking, we fear coming to the end of our finite existence — there's the loss of ourselves in this life, and that's it.

But actually, endings establish new relationships. People fear endings because they must surrender their power in the world. But the other side of endings is the gateway to new power and new relationships, to a new way of being in the world. Dying is a new way of way of being in the world. An ending establishes a relationship between ourselves and the unknown.

I had a client who was born in Germany and grew up in Europe. After World War II he went to C.G. Jung to work on some problem. But Jung told him "I can't take you, I'm not taking any more patients, I'm preparing to die." This was about one year before Jung died. From this story I recognize that Jung knew his life well. He needed time to let his process come to its end. He knew how to be with his life. He knew how to make his end, and he lived that end completely.

Dying with Ed

I recall a friend of mine dying when we were both seventeen. He died of cancer. I remember how the gang would all gather together and make mass marches on the hospital ward, as though our very energy and determination would effect his cure. I remember the enforced visiting hours, and the stupid behavioral straight jacket they put my friend in and that we put ourselves in. Everybody knew he was dying. But they forced him to eat hospital food, when all he wanted was a hot pastrami sandwich which we sneaked in to him. I remember him sneaking smokes too, because they weren't permitted. Dying for him was the same rebellion against the prison of helplessness that was around him from his childhood on.

It wasn't until I took care of a patient who had cancer, many years later, that I really grasped Ed's dying and my relationship to it. When I worked with this woman, she told me about the feelings and thoughts, the resentments and hates

that she had and that she had had all her life. The
resentment she felt at being cheated by life, by
having many mothers, by being shipped from
one family to another. The experiences she told
me about were like a can of black worms in her
chest. When I looked at her chest, I saw deflation
and defeat. Slowly as she began to breathe easier
she told me she felt defeated because she never
could get what she wanted. A deep yearning that
frightened me appeared in her eyes and she said
to me, "I want what you have." She clutched me
to her breast, clutched me tight, with fear. She
told me that she was never taken care of, that she
could never get this kind of warmth that she
craved. I understood her style of dying, which
was to shrink in defeat and hopelessness. Her
death was a protest over the lack of love for her in
the world. That each of her three marriages, all
ending in failure, were turning points. Now, she
was literally wishing not to live.

I remembered then that Ed had lost his father two years before his own dying — a man he
was deeply attached to. He never mourned his
father. He just became delinquent, dropped out
of school and haunted pool rooms. Nobody made
the connection. Ed's way of dying, congealing
and shrinking, with his unspoken resentments at
feeling fatherless, manifested as brave stoicism.
And he died.

I remember all of us — his friends, his brother, his mother — bravely living the pretense of his getting well. I remember the jokes we made to cheer him up. The brave, smiley stuff. Then we would all agonize outside his room. We shared the terrors of his fate but couldn't express our fears. I have often wondered if my friend died thinking we really didn't care or couldn't feel. Even as I tell this story I begin to feel sad at not sharing his fear with him, and my fear with him. Maybe I am now finally ending something that has remained unended for 25 years. We cared Ed. We cared but we were scared. We missed you. We were frightened and angry. For me, there is still an empty space.

Recently I read in the newspaper about a remarkable young poetess who died of cancer. It is interesting that her death was reported as occuring "somewhere between one and two o'clock." Nobody was precise about it. Her husband sat next to her singing and reading her favorite poems. Her children went to school that day. The family had faced her coming death for many weeks. The woman died at home, quietly, without heroic measures.

How I wish we could have sung with Ed. How I wish we could have shared with Ed his dying, instead of pretending to fantasies. I don't know what you looked like when you died, Ed, or what you had to say. None of us did. We were all wrenched from you by established procedure. We were helpless in our fear. You had physical pain; we had emotional pain. You felt cheated at losing your young life; we felt cheated at losing you, and because something in us was dying. But none of this was expressed, not one word. We were too terrified. We saw your dying and we knew our fate. We acted on the surface of life; we never shared our emotional spaces. We masked our anger, our helplessness, our fear, our pain.

Most of us were relieved when Ed finally died. The burden of his suffering was gone, and the burden of ours as well. There were unspoken feelings of excitement among the gang. We could bind ourselves to the living once again. During Ed's dying we felt ourselves more intensely than we had in a long time. We especially felt our bodies and our fragility.

What a turning point this was for me. What I was asked to sacrifice was my innocence, and my unknowing. I was shocked that the young died, that death was so close to me. The roles we played were so naked — I, Ed and the family. And how we all played them out to the bitter end. This was not true in the case of the poetess, whose husband read and sang to her, and whose family participated in her dying. In medieval Europe, many times dying took place in public. Friends and passersby would crowd into the dying person's room.

But when the time came in Ed's funeral proceedings, they asked all his friends to carry the coffin to the hearse. We were all sitting in the front row. I couldn't get up and do it, though other friends did. I didn't go to the cemetery. A friend and I walked home together forming our images of what death and dying was like. We talked about how creepy it was to be near the dead one, about there being nothing after death, about how death was an enemy that attacked and how one always had to be on guard. Most deaths were like executions; people were just waiting. These thoughts mobilized us against the aging process. And we cursed dying among strangers, and hoped our deaths would come quickly and without our knowing. We began to write Ed off into forgetfulness. I forgot to say goodbye, Ed.

Big dying evokes little dying. Ed's dying broke up the gang, forced each one of us back onto ourselves for the duration. Ed's death was a relief, a relief from the intensity of our emotional spaces, but not a relief from unendedness, which has continued for me to this day. Ed was a broken connection in my life until this writing.

Ed had physical pain, and the pain of the loss of his life. We could see it on his face, and it terrified us. We had emotional pain and the secret fear of suffering as Ed suffered. Ed's dying evoked in me my dread of pain and I responded to him from that dread. All this was part of the silent conversation in his hospital room. One time Ed communicated to us about the intensity of his physical pain. After that, we avoided letting him do that. There were things I had to discover about pain, and about its connection to helplessness. I think basically the fear of pain is the fear of being overwhelmed by it. Of being made helpless. Of helplessness without humanity.

Ed's mother used to moan and moan, outside his hospital room, moaning about giving up a relationship in her life that already didn't exist anymore. She couldn't yet conceive her relationship to life without Ed. Ed was unprepared to face the loss of himself — his long stay in the hospital, in the bed, didn't help. Once he was diagnosed and put into that hospital room, Ed became, to the established procedure, just another dying person. He had to face what every dying person faces — a situation in which their normal daily activity is interrupted, converted into their dying activity, which is their life at that point. Ed was never able to come to terms with the loss of his life. Nobody talks about this but dying persons end up being dead before they are dead. They are alienated, cut off from social reality. They are our living dead.

Since Ed's dying, and other peoples' I have witnessed and shared, I have gradually allowed the unexpressed to emerge from me. I more and more experience myself — my terror, my sense of loss, my excitement and curiosity, my help-lessness, my anger, my pain, and the intensity of my contact. I have permitted myself to learn from these experiences. Every person's dying is a model for our dying. Every person's dying is emotional learning. Nature teaches us about our dying through empathy and through example. "We are all born dying." Formerly dying was more of a family and a tribal event than it is now, an event in which the mysteries of this primary experience enriched people's lives.

Most of us die a tame death, leaving no trace of our conception of life and death. But I have a friend who died of leukemia. He could not make peace with his dying; he broke up the hospital room a couple of times. Even an acid trip (LSD) did not help. Everybody said he was infantile. But it was only in this way that he made some peace. He saw that he didn't have to die silently, so he died protesting. He shocked that hospital in Salt Lake City because he would not "behave himself." He wouldn't resign himself. As Dylan Thomas wrote: "Do not go gentle into that good night, / Rage, rage against the dying of the light."

For some people complaining and screaming and raging is a part of living their dying. For others, it may be just to talk openly about their fears, their ideas, their perceptions and to remain part of the family structure. I knew a man who came to me very upset over the death of his wife. He had wanted to try to maintain contact with her to the very end. But he felt her slipping away, until her speech seemed completely crazy. Just before she died she began to ask for change so that she could catch the bus. She kept asking her husband for change. He was dumbfounded and didn't know what to do.

People call it delirium or the effect of drugs, but I see that the body in that near-death situation is continuing to live its process and is not particularly threatened, even though the doctors and the friends are.

Perhaps the woman's request was symbolic. Perhaps change to catch the bus was her request to make an end, her request for permission to die. What would have happened if the husband had attempted to enter his wife's world by giving her, verbally or with gestures, or however, the change?

I was working with a friend one time in a workshop. He looked right at me and said he felt like fainting. He simply said, "I feel like fainting." I said, "Go ahead." And he did. He just fainted right there. There were no previous signs that he was pale or faint. He said he felt like fainting, so I gave him permission.

A friend of mine doing research with comatose patients in a V.A. hospital told me that patients in comas used to be treated as if they were dead. Everything around them was quiet and sterile. This belief, that comatose patients are dead, is no longer held to be true. The therapy now is to put these people in the halls, where passersby are encourage to touch them, and to play the radio for them. This change in attitude is a recognition that a comatose person is alive and responsive to others and to their environment.

It is commonly held that our body is some kind of dumb animal or brute from which the mythical "person" has to be protected. As if the body can't respond. As if intelligence, awareness and understanding were not its property too. As if the body were a piece of meat. The body has the right to end itself with its own intelligence. Nothing less.

We rob ourselves, our culture and the dying

of experiences that can tell us so much about how life terminates, about the nature of human experience in this part of the life process, about possible social roles, about visions and inner conflicts, about self-formativeness, about how self-affirmation diminishes or continues in dying and about the nature of our universe from the viewpoint of this stage of our process. In effect, we have disconnected ourselves from the dying and frightened ourselves until we're left without the hope of a myth, and without true knowledge.

Socrates, when asked what he wanted on the last day of his life, replied: "Since I have neglected the artist in me, I wish to live this last day as an artist."

A black intern at the county hospital now watched Mary Young die of pneumonia.

The intern did not know her. He had been in Midland City for only a week. He wasn't even a fellow American, although he had taken his medical degree at Harvard. He was an Indaro. He was a Nigerian. His name was Cyprian Ukwende. He felt no kinship with Mary or with any American blacks. He felt kinship only with Indaros. As she died Mary was alone on the planet as were Dwayne Hoover and Kilgore Trout. She had never reproduced. There were no friends or relatives to watch her die. So she spoke her very last words on the planet to Cyprian Ukwende. She did not have enough breath left to make her vocal chords buzz. She could only move her lips noiselessly.

Here is all she had to say about death: "Oh my, oh my."*

Breakfast of Champions, Kurt Vonnegut, Dial Press/Seymour Lawrence, 1973. p. 64.

Mythologizing

Mythology is man's conceptualization of the unmapped sea of human experience. Mythologizing is making a story in order to derive meaning from our experiences. It is storytelling. Our myths are the private stories we tell ourselves about what has happened to us. In this section I explore how we mythologize our little dyings. I explore the process of how we disorganize ourselves, how we break our boundaries and how our little dyings allow the emergence of the unknown.

A Base for Myth

Experience is connected to myth. Being immersed in self-experience is living one's own myth, one's own life story. Each time we reflect on what we have experienced we are creating a story to explain that experience or we are accepting someone else's explanation of it: our parents', our teacher's, the boss's, our spouse's, the culture's. This created story or explanation influences how we will react to similar situations in the future, how we live our lives and how other people learn from us. The making of the story or explanation is how we transfer new experience to ourselves and to other members of the tribe. In this book I talk about how to make a new story or myth about dying, how to become immersed in experience so that each of us can create his own story about dying. At each turning point we have a chance either to make a new myth for ourselves or to follow an old one. Being immersed in self-experience allows the alternative of the new.

When we mourn, when we dream, when we paint a picture or compose a poem, we are participating in an inner dialogue, a process in which ordinary social awareness has been limited or surrendered in favor of another awareness. We may decide to attend the dying, sleep, paint or write, but the expression of mourning, dreaming or artistry that results is not controlled by or derived from ordinary awareness. It flows from other aspects of the self. The decision to dream, for instance is not made from ordinary awareness; the decision to sleep is. Sleeping is one way to set up conditions or boundaries within which the self dialogue called dreaming can take place. Sleep may make dreaming as a bodily event possible, but it does not determine just when or what one dreams.

Process is the continual ongoingness of our lives that is manifest as movement, experience, knowing. We can identify process at work through such rhythmic activities as breathing in and breathing out, going to sleep and waking up, getting hungry and feeling satisfied, growing tired and feeling rested, and increasing sexual desire that leads to orgasm.

Viewed as process, dying is a continuation of living. We can be said to have a dying plan or program as surely as we had a birth program.

Dying is the precondition on which birth is available to us. Birth is a statement about the dying of the uterine life. All growth stages, all turning points, are a dying.

However, the program for dying, like the programs for mourning, dreaming, exhaustion, artistic expression, breathing, sleeping, hunger, sexuality and so many others, is not readily available to ordinary awareness. These programs, these scripts, are not subservient to social control, but are co-equal with it and influence its functioning. They cannot be produced or evoked upon demand. To the extent that they can be made available at all, they must be approached through their own idiom, through the discovery of their expression as a non-verbal language in daily life.

In other words, we can't practice dying by doing exercises for it. Exercises, mental or physical, are deliberate constructs designed to accomplish a goal or solve a problem. They impose their own demands onto the body's process. Gestalt techniques, psychodrama and bio-energetics, for example, can be very useful in resolving conflicts about social roles or personal definitions of self. But the problem really is more than the resolution of conflicts. It is making our processes more available in our everyday experiencing.

The act of living gives ample opportunity to become familiar with the ways we are dying. Our dying's significance is related to the unfolding of the life we create. As our connectedness to living deepens, we learn that experience is the teacher. And experience cannot be programmed. We are our own mythmakers, knowingly or unknowingly.

Social Images and Self Images

Our visualizations — the pictures we see in our mind's eye — can be divided into outer images, which have their basis in social mythology, and private, self-generated images, which are expressions of our somatic life. Since breathing is intimately associated with self activity, I use it to evoke images and feelings. So I conceived the idea of breathing in halves. When I do this experiment, I take a series of five breaths sequentially and with each inhalation reduce how much air I take in to one-half the previous breath's amount. I pause briefly at the end of each exhalation and inhibit the urge to inhale.

After the fifth breath, I yawn and allow my breathing to return to normal, trying to experience the sensations that I feel. I find that there are several levels to this experience. One part of me says "Breathe! Breathe! Breathe! You keep this up you're going to die!" But then there is also a kind of excited darkness, located in my torso, another kind of awareness altogether. It is quite different from my anxiety message. One part of me is afraid of dying while another part is excited. As I do this experiment a little longer, I begin to feel a wash of sensations, carrying with it memories and visions.

I recognize that the anxiety message is my survival mechanism. "Breathe! Breathe! Take in more air!" But the feeling of excited darkness carries a message "Don't stop!" I take this apparent contradiction to mean that not all of me is afraid of dying. Part of me is anxious, but part of me is excited.

Transcending rational awareness is like dying, it's coming around to another level of experience. There is a part of me that says I'm afraid of dying, but which part is it? Part of me is excited and feels pleasure if I initiate the threat of dying.

Images can be pictures or they can be concepts meant to convey patterns of feelings and sensations. Concepts from the culture can inhabit us, telling us who we are. They seem then to spring forth from within us as if they were our own. Also, through exposure to the media, and from hearsay, we receive many morbid or horrible images about dying, and these are always the first to come up when we encounter feelings of anxiety or of fear.

On the other hand, feelings and emotions may be described as spontaneous self images that are quite different from social images. Genuine self images are biological expressions and may not be visually oriented — for example, feelings of beauty, grace, shyness, awkwardness.

On the basis of their images, people say, "Dying is painful" and "Death is bad, to be avoided at all costs." But my breathing experiment convinces me that I can have some experiences with initiating my dying program that are not negative.

Changes in the body chemistry can alter images. In my breathing experiment I increased the amount of carbon dioxide in my bloodstream, and immediately triggered anxiety and images of dying. All emotional, bio-chemical environments have their concomitant images and feelings. For example, a feeling of sadness may trigger sensations of choking and the image of being smothered, or rage may trigger sensations and images of annihilation.

Dying poses the danger of the loss of my life as I have come to know it. But I have learned to ask, which part of me is feeling the loss? Is it the organic self? Is it my ego, my conscious self? Is it the social me that is afraid, that says, "I won't be here anymore"? Which part of me is threatened by my images of dying?

After listening to many people tell me about their images of dying, I began to see that fears always fell into either of two categories — social or personal. The death you die is the life you live. The more you choose to live your life ouside the culture's images, the more you will die outside those images too. When I asked myself "How am I afraid to die?", I had images of dying in the social category — from the culture's programs — and they were violent images. "I don't want to be run over by a truck." "I don't want to be shot." "I don't want to die in surgery." And so on.

Images of dying tend to be confused with feelings of dying. When looking at ways we are afraid to die, images may come up that cause intense anxiety. The message of anxiety is that something is dangerous, one may die. At that moment, the threat and the feeling of dying are intertwined, are the same. However, the feeling of dying itself has not caused the anxiety; it's the image of dying that has.

If you're afraid of being suffocated, you may evoke an image of drowning, or of being stranded. Any event that triggers your images of dying will automatically trigger the anxiety of dying. At that moment you feel you may die. You are anxious, you are panicked, you feel you may die. So you come to associate the anxiety you feel with what dying will be like. You tell yourself dying will be like this. "I'm very anxious and afraid. Dying makes me anxious and afraid. This is what dying is like; it's like what I am feeling right now." But that may not be so.

I discovered in the breathing experiment that I could experience both anxiety and excitation around an event because different levels of me responded simultaneously in different ways. It is also true that our thoughts about dying can be different from our feelings about dying. The feelings can be sensuous and the thoughts can be quite frightening. I don't want to oversimplify thoughts and feelings about dying, because there are many other things to consider about them, but I want to drive home the point that it's quite common to experience a contradiction between thoughts of dying and feelings of dying.

When I ask myself, "How am I afraid to die?" I try to evoke my images of dying and death, either through the breathing experiment or through my imagination. Then I separate the feelings these images have from the images themselves. I might hold them in my consciousness, remember them or draw them, write them down, to look at them without quite so much panic or stereotyped reactions. I contemplate my reactions, my responses. Most of these images are of violent deaths, the kind pictured in the newspapers and on television everyday. I look at them and say to myself, "Dying may *not* be like this," because I know I am picturing to myself the cultural images of dying. Violence is, after all, almost all we see of dying. I go through this same process with my dreams.

The culture, in general, favors eruptive dying, but it is possible to die congealingly instead. Harry Truman did. All societies control dying styles by putting positive values on certain programs, including many that can be personally negative. For example, our society does not devalue dying by murder. It doesn't come right out and say that, but underneath a high value is placed on many forms of violent dying. The society is programming its members to die quickly, suddenly, by another hand. It's advantageous because it's very quick. Orgastic, explosive, and bang, boom, no helpless lingering, no problems taking care of you, no cost, no dependency, no

remorse, nothing. Life is simply interrupted, bang! A quick dying takes away the need for a geriatric program or for a social state, and it does away with the many expensive problems of lingering convalescence. Individuals support quick dying programs because they do away with personal problems of remorse, and minimize mourning.

We all live in the mind of the culture, and I don't mean that derogatorily. We don't realize that we are living out somebody else's dying program. We don't realize we may be living out their life programs as well. We think we are exercising free choice but we unerringly choose the culture's programs. We think that's all there is to choose from. So we end up not living our own life, and then dying someone else's death.

What dying is natural to people? Nobody knows but everyone has images of it, and everyone is partly afraid of dying unnaturally. For my purposes, natural dying is one that can be lived as a continuation of one's style of life, a dying that is not an interruption to but rather an extension of one's life.

People who have vested their energy in eating well, exercising mind and body with yoga, body therapies, spiritual practices and alternate relationships, have chosen another way of living and another way of dying. They seem to wish to avoid the common cultural deaths — cancer or heart disease. People who find themselves outside of the culture because of their age also have a chance to create a new lifestyle and a new dying style.

Families that hold their emotional ties together have made decisions not to die alone. Families that break apart easily or that have no emotional ties institute anxiety about dying alone among their members. Dying is a personal, but also a family and a tribal, process.

Making Your Experience Count — Becoming Somebody

People don't remember being born. They just know they are alive, and it seems as though they have always been alive. It has never been any different in the world than it is now.

What do you imagine death is? How do you come to grips with the fact of dying? Do you avoid it, admit it? Connecting with feelings about dying is a step in breaking through the cultural images, and in building a new mythology for yourself.

I ask myself, do I share my dying with other people? Do I talk about it or keep silent? Am I reluctant, am I guarded, do I feel ashamed? What kind of talking about dying do I do with myself? Do I write myself letters? Pass notes under the table? Send myself messages I can't decipher, notes written with invisible ink? Do I experience these thoughts and these feelings or inhibit them, postpone, distort, reject them? Do my thoughts, feelings, images, memories link up, creating an interconnected me?

A man in real estate once told me that several years previous he had had a hemorrhage and was taken to the hospital, where they told him: "Friend, you have a very strong chance of dying." When this realization became clear to him, his ambiguity was decreased. My friend said all of a sudden he felt, wow, he felt free. He said his body was flooded with excitement and that he felt charged to the gills. It was completely crazy, paradoxical. He said for the first time in his life he felt free to feel lost, without rules. And he looked forward to it with excitement. He said for the first time he could really enjoy life with no responsibilities. I suggested to him that that may have been why he got well. For the first time he could commit himself to what he wanted rather than to social pretending.

I was in a propeller-driven airplane once when all four engines went out. Before we landed, I had enough time to prepare myself to die. It wasn't very long but it was long enough. And a number of incredible things happened to me. The first thing was that I became transparent to myself, through being flooded with excitement. It broadened me, deepened me, bang, some space opened up. I felt that my head was full of panic. I felt panic in my brain, my eyes, and in my face. But below my neck there was no panic. I

was super-charged — there was adrena-
line — but I was calm as a donut.

I don't remember the sequence, though I've
been over it a hundred times, but I was flooded
with a sense of who I was. I can't explain that to
you except to say that I was filled with a kind of
inknowing — I was filled from inside out with
an overwhelming sweetness and light, but it
wasn't like a visible light. I was filled with
acceptance and love for myself. I had a taste of
being full of myself, of having filled myself with
my excitement. I was fully immersed in myself,
and I was abundant, everything was okay. From
then on, my whole life was re-oriented. I was
thirty-one at the time, and I recall the experience
for you as another example of the contradictions
that can exist when making connections with
dying.

We live in an age in which everyone is wanting more and more responsibility for everything
in their lives. Why not carry this responsibility
over to dying? You will not die until all of you de-
cides to. You are intimately involved with the
process of decision-making for your own life
and therefore for your own dying. This
responsibility does not manifest on a cognitive
level alone, or even primarily.

When we try to control life and dying from the cognitive level we end up denying both life and death, living beside life, not in it. No one says this, but most people are not immersed in life, and they know it. They contract themselves, accept social roles as the reality and try to live successfully within this limitation.

The character of our life is the character of our dying; both are part of one process. Many people withdraw from life, yet they don't want to die. They don't want to participate in the dying process any more than they want to participate in the living process.

In our culture living is lopsided. The brain is kept alive and the body ignored. The life of the mind is valued, that of the body denigrated. We live only a part of our self, a part of our bodies, a part of our feelings, a part of our existence. We need to take ourselves seriously, making our life the starting point, making our experience count. By doing so, we become somebody.

In the process of becoming somebody, the ground of the mystery of existence is revealed — the experience which no one can tell us about. Each person discovers the terms of his own aliveness, and his own dying. Many people accept dying by perceiving that there is a great difference between their images or their thoughts of dying and their feelings about it. To hold on to our images can perpetuate fearfulness. Clinging to our thoughts can make them morbid and defeating or unpleasureable. Taking ourselves seriously thrusts us directly into life and a new reality of our own dying.

We live two different ways — a social life and a personal life, a public life and a private one. The social life encompasses the impressions and images of programmed social patterns. It gives acceptance and roles. The private self grows out of body processes and impressions. In most of us one or the other dominates. Generally, self-identity and a sense of continual self-realization is formed publicly. It is difficult for most people to mature in our society with a well-formed self-generated vision.

I have slowly come to understand that most people are not frightened of dying, but are afraid of being killed. The most serious unanswered question for people about dying is how they feel about being killed, about their helplessness. I see that ultimately every fear of being punished, of being ostracized, or being alienated, of not getting approval, always boils down to the fear of being killed. "What do you mean, your mother won't like you, what will happen?" "I'll be alone, nobody will take care of me." "Well, then, what will happen?" "I'll be hungry with nothing to eat." "So? Then what will happen?" "So, then I will be helpless. And left to die." Are not all forms of discipline basically a threat to living? And what is anxiety, but the dread that something will happen, be done to us, we will be killed? It is this victim's role that terrorizes.

Think back to your childhood days, when you were small. Just at the beginning of memory. Was it not this helplessness that provoked feelings of terror?

Deciding to connect with feelings of dying is making a commitment to the unknown. The courage that is needed may simply be the courage of looking at your assumptions about dying. Or to create your own myth. This could result in experiences no one has told you about.

From all the recorded experiences of people who have nearly died by drowning, airplane accidents, great falls, or in other ways, but who survived, the one consistent feature has been that their experience was completely different from their expectations, and completely outside ordinary images about dying.

Living your dying is to live your life, trusting your experiences. Being somebody is different from being nobody.

The Threat of Not Existing

Most of us tend to project our social roles into the future in the hopes of keeping the future stable. It is these socialized roles that we fear losing because we equate them with existing. To lose our roles is to fear losing our continuity. Futurizing is part of living. The projection of ourselves into the future extends our existence and guarantees the continuity of our on-goingness. Generally whatever inhibits our thrust to the future causes fear. We cannot imagine a space in which there is no longer a personal identity. We fear not existing whether we know it or not. We simply have no frame of reference for it.

Dying may be the unwillingness or inability to integrate new experiences and new form, the cessation of expansion and contraction. Biological life, for me including the psychological existence, has three major concerns. One is to maintain itself. Another is to expand itself. And the third is to replicate itself. Whatever threatens

any one of these threatens the continuity of existence, causes anxiety. What threatens to break
the thread of continuity is like the fear of non-ex-
istence. It equals the fear of being killed. We feel
discontinuity will kill us. Most people respond
to a loss of continuity with fears of dying. Life,
however, is discontinuous. For reasons of
security and the maintenance of social roles
everyone tries to ignore feelings of discontinuity. Even when we go to sleep each night we
affirm our identities by maintaining our
accepted ways of imaging, reviewing our day or
projecting an exciting or meaningful problem to
solve tomorrow.

The first thing when we get up in the morning we're thinking about that problem or about
getting breakfast, or about being a beautiful
woman, or any of a whole stream of actions and
thoughts which organize our self-identity and
our reference to the world. In this way we permit
no loss of continuity and self-reference through
sleep.

I go to bed telling myself that I am a writer
and I wake up thinking about writing books. The
memory of our lives is the attempt to keep an
unbroken stream of feelings, thoughts, and actions going. We want to believe our lives are totally continuous. We don't remember too much

about the empty spaces. We think we're absent-minded or forgetful when we hit the empty spaces. A moment of discontinuity is like loss, with all its emotional responses, which may be equated with dying.

Imagine you're in a dark room, alone. All of a sudden where before you could see nothing someone has put the light on. You don't know where you are. Someone opens the door, someone you've never seen. They call you by the wrong name and insist that that's your name. They insist you are in a place you never heard of, where you have never been before. What does that feel like?

What happens when you don't recall an event? What has happened? Have you lost your sense of continuity? All of a sudden you experience a gnawing doubt that a bridge in your awareness is not there. Connectedness is broken. You were in a place you can't remember, doing something you don't recall. You may begin to doubt who you really are, or where you are. Your entire existence is threatened.

This imagined loss of continuity is really a loss of social orientation, which is one of the primary losses everyone dreads. This continuity is the glue that holds our social fabric together.

This contract of accepted roles is maintained by feelings, and if this is impossible, through thought or action or sometimes sensation. Any threat to one of these connections causes anxiety and leads us to withdraw or to reinforce the ways we know we can stay connected.

An experience outside the culture's way of experiencing, if told to others, is usually unacceptable, or makes us feel alien. This becomes equal to being crazy, or cut off, not connected to the culture — dead. Many science fiction films play on this point, when people think the hero is nuts who sees a giant bug. Discontinuity is the feeling of being unattached, disembodied from the cultural body. It is the threat of not existing, of being dead.

Each of us has the ability to end our own existence, socially or bodily. In surrendering social identity and continuity, perhaps we enter a new experience of existence.

How far does your life space extend? I live in Berkeley. I feel my life space pervading my house, my office. Beyond the house, it extends to local buildings where I give workshops or speak regularly. Since I am affiliated with the Esalen office in San Francisco, my life space easily extends there by telephone. I also give workshops in Chicago, Toronto, Boston and San Diego.

Through memory, experience, personal friend-
ships and the telephone, I am constantly in contact with a real sense of the extent of my life
space — it spans the continent.

Dying is the loss or the changing of those
boundaries. Dying is the surrendering of values
and ways that make up our world. The dying
process does not have to be slowing down,
shrinking back, understanding and accepting reduced contact. But surely it is the world op-
erating differently. You've got to be prepared for
an entirely different world, for new possibilities.

Allowing our boundaries to change is akin
to being alone. Being without the old ways.
Being alone is facing the unknown for most people. Being alone is solitude, but it is not neces-
sarily loneliness. Being alone can lead to the es-
tablishment of a new relationship with oneself.
Many of us, through chronic contraction of our
bodies or our imagination, never permit ourselves a new sense of existence. We use our contractions to cement our boundaries, to try to
guarantee our continued existence. Dying is the
crack in our boundaries that leads to a new existence.

Facing the Unknown

There are images from our observations and from our memories that we believe are painful or terrible. These are mostly mutilation scenes. And there are feelings that we fear. These are mostly feelings that are unusual or unfamiliar to us. What is the feeling of dying like?

I recall in the early days of my work that when people opened themselves to painful psychological spaces, and their bodies contorted, I was frightened. There was one chap who collapsed on the floor before me — writhing, screaming and crying incoherently. I thought his pain was enormous. My fear was. It almost robbed him of his experience. Later he assured me that it was not so painful. I learned from this and subsequent experiences that my imagination of his pain was mine.

People say they have a feeling of dying, but I think they have a feeling they attribute to not existing. They experience a feeling unfamiliar or frightening to them and they associate it with the possibility of not existing. The image of dying, at least in our culture, is so overloaded with terror and panic that it is difficult to get at what the pure feeling of dying or the pure feeling of what the process of death might be. When we talk of the fear of dying we are only able to say that well people — persons not in the dying process — are terrified of it.

Once in a group a young man described to me his absolute terror when, in the middle of the night, he was awakened by an image of a man in his room. This image, this apparition, was ghost-like and filmy in appearance. The young person said he knew this image was not real, was apparently a projection of his own mind, but at the same time he was terrified of it. If in his situation he could have permitted this image of terror, and not been victim to it, he would have made a discovery that ranks at the very top of the discoveries of men — that he has the power to resist non-being. We all do.

I was talking recently with a woman who worked with geriatric patients. She told me that many of the patients know they're dying. "They have such beautiful fantasies of what their world is going to be." I said to her, "Listen, Paula, what do you mean fantasies? They describe a place, a feeling, a particular kind of reality. And you call it a fantasy! What you're really saying is that their description doesn't fit your perception of what the world is like. What you've done is put the dying person outside of your frame of reference, and say that their world doesn't exist. You turn their perception into an hallucination!"

That's a terrifying position to any person, but especially to the dying person, since it teaches them to reject their own perceptions. The dying person speaks of a place they are sensing, or feel they are moving toward, They may be in a certain psychic state, but then that state causes their social alienation. The result is a loss of inner continuity that is fearful.

I was sitting in a chair with my eyes half open, letting in just a little light, and I began to imagine a point or fantasize a tiny object at a distance beginning to move closer and closer to me. I let it grow in size until it became much larger as it approached. I wanted to see what reactions I would have. When it grew huge, I felt I was being overwhelmed. If I conceive of death as coming at me like this I am terrified. But death does not come to get me. I am it. As I sat during this game the panic I felt was connected to my conception of dying, but it wasn't connected to the dying process. The panic originated in my images.

Birthing can be painful event, which the mother and child register and remember. I think that if a mother has deep inhibitions against experiencing her own pleasure and is afraid of her child's birth, even though she desires it and wants it, then the child mobilizes against the uterine resistance. I think many people walk around with bodily memories of their birth which act as a trigger for anxiety about dying. A child having to push itself through a contracted opening into the world has memories of this struggle cellularly implanted. Or it may be that a normally tight, small pelvis may present difficulties to the child that are painful and traumatic. Also, a mother's previous experience with this difficulty may predispose her to fear normal birthing pressure, and contract.

This creates a binding effect on the body which inhibits expansion. The fear is that we may not live, and a kind of helplessness. In this way being born and dying are organismically similar events.

To clarify, though, we do not have to die helplessly, any more than the child is consciously worried about the constricted passage. It's too deeply involved in the process for that. However, this does not prevent the organism from perceiving and registering the event in such a way as to create a deep fear of it. The bodily effects of a constricted birth may act as a self-inhibiting factor during life.

I believe that when a child is born the outside of the mother's body becomes an extension of the womb. The rhythmic, pulsatory patterns of the womb are continued, albeit modified, on the surface of the mother's body. When the child is taken from the mother and incubated, stress patterns of breathing are instituted and the child is alienated. This action mobilizes anxiety in the new body and a deep fear is built into it from that point. Later on, as the organism begins to die, that fear returns, since the organism may tend to die as it was born or to act in such a way as to avoid the experience of its birth. The dying person experiences fears that they will again be constricted and alienated and helpless.

In this sense of alienation, of the pressure of constriction, of loss, of surrendering roles to the dying process, feelings may begin to emerge that are negative, hostile, revengeful, sadistic. The dying person's self-image alters. You have an image of being a good person who never gets angry. All of a sudden anger and hatred is mobilized in you, apparently from nowhere. You can't deal with it. So you try to block it, to push it back inside, but that becomes painful. Or you want to scream like you weren't allowed to scream as a kid. "Don't leave me alone! Don't desert me! Don't take me away from contact because it scares me!" But you're not supposed to do that; you're supposed to be brave, to be self-sufficient. You're supposed to die silently, without giving anybody any trouble — just the way you have lived. And so you relive all the fears of childhood and never protest.

These things must come up. They lie at the base of all our fears of dying — that we will have to face again the unresolved anxieties and fears of our early lives. And our institutions try to force us to resolve these feelings the way we had to resolve them in childhood. "You must learn to be alone. And to die alone. To die without friends and to die by yourself." Which is the whole thing you have been warding off all your life.

Dying is having to face the unknown in a world controlled so thoroughly that unknowns are only fearful experiences. Our society is the on-going result of a history of working hard to control unknowns. In one lifetime there are tremendous strides toward such control.

However, Unknown with a capital U is the central fact of life. Whatever the qualities and activities are by which we make life seem to be a continuity of aware activity, these are the controls by which we attempt to eliminate the Unknown. Living your dying is facing the Unknown. There's a conflict between the objective reality we want to establish and live out and the subjective reality that motivates us. Objective reality is arrived at by a social concensus about inner reality. We agree that such and such a thing is something we have all experienced, and therefore it's real. Science is based on this logic, and so is the life of the culture.

A large part of what one calls unknowns simply are the normal events of deeper experience. Beyond this, one has to recognize that life reveals itself in its own way, a way quite foreign to the reasoning process that organizes and controls objective reality.

What does it mean to lose control? Our acquisitive and possessive education makes us ward off all loss. We have to be forced to give something up. This acquisitive mentality is deeply rooted in all our activity. One consequence is a secret fear in everyone that letting go ultimately means the loss of control over bladder and bowels. The fear of this possibility, the shame this "accident" creates, is due to the ostracization in our society this crime brings immediately on the head of anyone over three or four years old. It is an example of feelings and experiences avoided or controlled all through life. The fear of inappropriate elimination is a powerful example of a whole family of hidden fears to be confronted. Other examples are: the fear of screaming; the fear of not knowing the right way to act; the fear that one won't be brave; the fear of displeasing someone in authority. All such fears arise out of individual and family applications of the cultural rules and can cause the dying person to die someone else's death rather than their own.

Norman O. Brown has said that only a person with unlived lives is afraid to die. A person who feels he has lived his life — the way he wanted — is not afraid. The fear of dying is tied to the goals of who you believe you have to be rather than who you are.

Part of the fear of dying, and of the excitement of living, arises because since we can conceptualize our future, we are subject to disappointments and catastrophes. The fear of dying can come from the loss of our futurized expectations. A part of living is learning how to correct some of our incorrect mythology as we go. Letting go of what we no longer need. This could include some of our futurizing.

In the later stages of dying there is sensation. There are no ideals, there are no concepts, there is simply the state of being in that process. And as I say this to you I don't believe I could have used these words except that I have been so much myself I have known times when I have lost my sense of my body. Once I got into this space I was alive without images. I lived with the strongest sense of being me.

Says I to Myself Says I

There are many ways to describe the path to dying. There is acceptable dying, unacceptable dying, natural dying and unnatural dying, accidental dying, sudden dying, surprise dying, passive dying, suicide, premature dying, diseased dying, self-destruction and the list could go on and on. Granted that different names could apply to similar styles for dying, all these terms reflect serious attempts to talk about and understand how and why people die and in what way a death connects to the life that preceded it.

Any distinct style for dying is really a program for dying. That is, it is part of a template or unfolding having roots far back into a person's life. Just as each personality is unique, so there is an infinite variety of styles for dying, but they do seem to conform to certain general characteristics. I already have described the two basic styles of dying, congealing and eruptive, resulting directly as a consequence of the energetic process. Within each style, one can distinguish whether a person dies his own unique death, one expressive of his person, or whether he dies someone else's, or the culture's.

In seminars on dying I have led, people almost always express some kind of regret for things they have not done in their lives, and specific fears connected to "bad" dying.

A good dying was usually described as either one having no pain or a "natural" death (old age, for example), and a bad dying was usually one no one wanted. People were willing to die, then, as long as their death was desirable.

Good and bad dying have also been expressed as "I want to die like a person with dignity, in control, not screaming or out of control in my emotions." These concerns with good and bad dying were expressed by those who did not want to know that they were dying. Usually they wished it to be quick, unexpected, a sudden fatal violence, an auto accident or a heart attack. These persons generally wished to do their dying alone, in private, without being prepared. There was conflict, though, between those who wished to die quickly or unprepared, say in their sleep, and the lack of a chance to say goodbye.

There were those who opted for more slow dying styles. They wished very much to participate, to see the end coming, to put their affairs in order, to have their friends and relatives around. They often spoke of wanting to melt into the universe, leak into it, drift away while being touched, held, or otherwise have contact. They were concerned to be alert yet without pain.

A person who is afraid to live their own dying might be willing to be killed in an airplane crash, an automobile wreck or in any number of ways in which they would be passive and without direct responsibility for their death. Also, since the culture generally approves of violent death, such a person would be living one form of the culture's death. This could be seen as the Grim Reaper — a form of the popular notion that death will come to get you — a medieval image that in a way gets fulfilled in the above example. I can get somebody to kill me. That's one expression of my desire not to die by myself or from my own hand. A variation would be dying from surgery; getting a doctor to kill me under the guise of attempting to save my life. This dying program follows the pattern: "I don't have to live my life, or my dying."

Premature dying is a program by which death seems to come before one's time. A twenty-three-year-old man develops bone cancer and is dead three weeks later. Or Jennie dies of leukemia in *Love Story*. Or an eighteen-year-old develops heart disease. All the deaths in this style seem to come as a result of the kind of disease you usually associate with a much older person.

The boundary between accidental dying and suicide is nebulous. There was a study made in Texas which showed that almost 30% of all automobile accidents may have been suicides. There were documented reports in this study like the following: A man, furious in an argument with his wife, said to her, "I wish I were dead." Minutes after he stormed out of the house and drove off in his car, he was dead. He apparently just drove in front of another car.

Likewise the boundary between accidental dying and voluntary, passive dying is unclear. Several years ago a French airliner went down near Dijon with fifty-five people on board. Four or five survived. One, an older Frenchman, was quoted as saying that he hadn't wanted to get on the plane. He knew something was not right. He ignored or overrode himself. He got a message that said to his conscious, decision-making self, "Don't get on that plane!" but he decided to go anyway.

I had an automobile accident once when I was in a state of anger. I was completely discombobulated. I was very intense, frustrated, and didn't know what to do about a situation I was in. And it later occurred to me that at that time self-destruction was a viable alternative.

I'm trying to show that styles of dying are manifestations of specific programs that can be at least partly understood. Sudden dying, for example, may be the result of not listening to one's subtle messages, coupled with the fact that in the situation dying is a viable alternative. I believe this means that the part of a person which ignores the warning message really wants to die. Perhaps because the person is frightened to be so much in contact with himself, or to think about dying as a possibility, he doesn't see the significance. A lot of sudden deaths may not be sudden deaths, but subtle suicides. We would normally think of them as accidental. But when a person "has an accident," say cutting his finger on a can he is opening, we realize that the accident is a result of the person not paying attention, and being out of contact with himself. The organism has somehow not bridged the gap between its normal level of coordination and the attempted action.

Also, of course, we don't know how any person is working out their dying program — what kind of dying that person wants. It may be that the sudden, seemingly accidental dying is just the dying that person seeks. This is not a morbid statement. Dying is a perfectly valid response to certain situations.

Balzac, in *The Alquest,* tells of a woman caught in a conflict between her children and her husband. She's torn between love and fidelity, and unable to know what to do. Finally, she calls her daughter to her and turns the responsibility for the husband over to the daughter. It becomes clear the wife is choosing to die as her solution to this conflict. This is astounding since Balzac paints it almost as a voluntary act. In the story, ending one's life voluntarily becomes a viable alternative.

There can be a willingness to die, a willingness to get life over. To be without passiveness. To be a victim of our dying process. For example, we might feel that a great injustice was done to us, and decide to hasten our dying. The willingness to die is related to the willingness to live life and to understand it in its own terms. Or it may be the willingness to resist it. The need to protest — to join our dying, instigate it, but then protest.

Willingness means the interaction, the cooperation, of all the parts of ourselves. It means a decision to make contact with any parts that are resistant. The instinctual self, the psychological self, the social self and the biological self beginning to be in a dialogue. The feeling self talking with the thinking self, or the acting self responding to the imaging self; dying part talking with living part, social part talking with body part. Out of this interaction can come a new understanding of our dying program as we work it out in our lives.

If you assume, as I do, that everyone is in some control of their own dying, it is possible to reach some familiarity with dying, and to learn how to gain more conscious direction over it by dialoguing with our less social selves and by learning to read our more interior messages.

When a physician finds evidence of cancer during an exam he never says to the patient "Something in you wants to die, something in you is against your social self or *for* your dying self." But that's the truth. There are plenty of people who have altered their dying programs and have gone on to live different lives. And there are plenty of people who choose consistently to ignore important aspects of their selves. I tend to put the businessman who keels· over at lunch with a heart attack and the delivery man who steps from behind his truck into the path of a car in this category. Such people are out of tune with themselves. They are not where they should be, either psychologically, physiologically or physically. The person is not fully in contact with himself, is not in the present, is off somewhere else. Many people simply have no idea that there are such things as deeper messages, that feelings and sensations are an integral part of self-experience. Many people believe dreams, fantasies, images, inner pictures and other spontaneous interior events have no purpose, meaning or usefulness to them. Such beliefs cut a person off from the tools, the concepts, the simple understandings that would allow him the choice to live independently from the culture's dictates, to be free to express who he wants to be.

But the real issue may be that dying is us — we die, we terminate ourselves. Nobody has to teach us how; we know how. In this sense each death is like a suicide. This may be our biggest secret. To know we know about dying, its how and maybe the when and the wish to live it, to have the opportunity for our own freedom.

Biological Time

1, 2, 3, 4, 5, 6 . . . the world is divided up into an infinite number of dots, of particles that can be measured to infinity. 23, 24, 25, 26, 27, and so on. This counting process, this continual addition of equal units, divides up time, divides up space. We take it for granted. We call it space time. But the culture needs linearity. It's a basic tool of the business and scientific world.

Supposedly this way of viewing space time — by measuring it in equal portions — had its popular beginning with the Renaissance. McLuhan says the invention of linear time goes along with the death of poetic language and the introduction of prose in our culture. In that era, a new accuracy was demanded and space and time as separate entities were established.

With this kind of world view we see the metering out of our lives. We see a beginning and we see an end. Events have to follow a certain course that is either finite or infinite. Then we're caught in an absolutely limited kind of thinking, which we could call *accounting time*. In this system, our calendar is rigid; our life is measured in equal doses and moves relentlessly forward to a finite conclusion. There can be no pause and no return.

However, there is another view we can hold. We can conceive of our life as *eventful*. We can become part of the process of life in terms of things occurring, of events and their expression. Events occur without a beginning or an end and can carry us to another level of existence entirely. Now I can talk about this occurrence in my life and that occurrence in my life, and I can begin to talk about ending my corporeal existence as a stage in my life. My personality is intimately linked to continuity. To expand or contract my personality is to alter this continuity. The concept of eventfulness allows us to surrender the culture's time and gain our own space time, an environment in which to live out our process.

Accounting time is imposed on our social selves; space time flows in the body self. Accounting time is based on machine precision; space time is biological, in which life is experienced as process. You could call space time body rhythms — which everyone knows about but few consider important. Let me point out that in space time one does not talk about the death of the body, but only the death of the body from the point of view of the observer. That's a wholly different phenomenon; it invites you to escape the culture by living your process, your self-experience from inside. I observe your dying. You may observe my dying. *But the experience of the process of dying has nothing to do with what you are observing.* If we derive our information about dying from our observations, we may have discovered nothing about what it is like to die.

When I give professional workshops, I have to remind those therapists over and over to focus on process. Forget product. We all are so attentive to accounting time and to cultural space that we ignore our deeper process of living. The culture values material over energy. Your task is to reverse this attitude in your life.

Living time is the time that it takes to become. It can be stated as the time of all the events that occur in our life expression. It doesn't really take nine months to hatch a baby. At the very least the space time involved has to include the span of the existence of the very first thought, the desire, the preparation of the uterus and the stretching or extending of space by people creating a new being. Our living is our life time.

Another differentiation is to distinguish so-cialized time from dying time. Socialized time is brain time, accounting time. Brain time is slower than hormonal time in the sense that a nerve im-pulse travels faster than your brain can think about it. Brain time is faster than hormonal in the sense that you can think faster than one feeling can develop fully in your experience. Molecular time is very fast, hundreds of times faster than brain time. However, on the organizational level, it takes millions of molecular events to produce one bodily event.

If you think of bodily functions as having a progressive value to the whole, then you see the brain function as more important than hormonal or molecular ones. This is evolutionary order, from single cell to man, held up to us in elemen-tary school. You decide thinking is more important than feeling. Such a valuative system is oriented sympathetically to the concepts of ac-counting time, end-pointing, product-oriented.

If you conceive of organismic functions as purely eventful, then you see the life of the organism engaged in continual self-expression between its many levels. It can be meaningful to describe brain, hormonal and molecular space times as equally important. Since we cannot die until all of us is willing, the dying process is a dialogue or monologue reconciling accounting time and the body's time.

Who is to say how long is a lifetime? Who is to say how long is dying time and what becomes of the space time world we have all agreed to accept? And why is the space time world of the dying, a lifetime in seconds of space, made unreal?

Sexuality

Sexuality is almost a training for dying — an intensification of the dying process and a rehearsal of the dying event. The orgastic state that produces feelings of ecstasy is a surrendering to the involuntary and to the unknown. Orgasm requires giving ourselves over to what is occurring in us. Our mundane awareness has to allow this surrendering. The orgastic state also produces feelings of dying, raises fears of dying, because the social awareness may be threatened by the involuntary. The build-up of excitation, the build-up of involuntary movement, the social awareness surrendering more and more to the dominance of the involuntary, then the peak, then the brief loss of consciousness which Wilhelm Reich describes as the feeling of being in the cosmos, without boundaries, without containment, and then the slow coming back is accompanied for many people by a fear of dying or a partial desire to avoid the experience. All descriptions I have read or heard of the orgastic state cite feelings of melting away, of being at one with, of not knowing where one has gone at a certain point. These reports, together with Reich's writings and my own experience have given me the clues that dying may be orgastic. There may be a link between dying and orgasm, dying and sexuality. How we allow or inhibit our orgastic experiences may be deeply related to our dying.

The orgastic model presupposes a build-up of energy until a peak is reached, discharge at the peak and then a diminution of energy. This model is achieved in the body through the combination of many rhythms coming together in harmony: the respiratory rate escalates; muscular coordination increases; the energy level increases; feelings and sensations are more intensely perceived. All these rhythms become more harmonious as they increase in intensity. They tend to sweep each other along, summating together. The rhythms of the body begin to find their way into the general pattern of excitation. Eventually there can be a unitary expression of the organism — complete involuntary participation in an event leading toward discharge.

The dying event is also the summation of many rhythms. But it's a kind of summation in reverse. The organism is in a continual state of excitation, but the amount of charge begins to even out. Expansion and contraction, inhalation and exhalation, excitation and diminution, opening up and closing down, illuminating the world then retreating to assimilate the world — all these biological patterns are evening out, becoming less and less close together. Many of the involuntary movements of the organism in the dying event, like defecation, getting an erection, body twitching, the tongue hanging out, the eyes rolling, are attempts to release energy, to give up excitation, to discharge, and allow the rhythms of life to find a continuum of expression. These rhythms seem arhythmical, disconnected; they do not summate together. Their pattern is the orgasmic pattern. Its outline can be seen even in sudden deaths.

Excitation, high-peaking, release in expression, assimilation, union — these stages are visible in every process of living. For example, fear is a high energy state that, true to this pattern, wants to come to completion. Therefore you don't explain fears away, you experience them, you integrate them, you let them go to their end. In the same way, pain, anxiety and other energy states can find resolution. The energy is expended in experiencing, fusion and completeness. We may be so attached to social or psychological roles that we may want to inhibit them from coming to an end. In this way, the high energy state — pain, terror, anxiety or whatever — is perpetuated. From this point of view — the energetic patterns of life — we can understand the necessity for endedness.

Looking at this process another way, I see that a woman who is pregnant always finds she is involuntarily preparing for birth. The organism deeply understands what to do. The whole body is programmed to make for pregnancy, for the growth of the fetus and for the eventual delivery of the child. Breathing patterns are prepared, stretching patterns are initiated, feeling responses change. The whole organism gears up for the event.

I think the same thing holds true in dying. The organism understands how to die. We can facilitate or inhibit the process. One of the interesting things is that the organism has a feedback mechanism for self-correction. We can learn to write another myth. We can play a part in the creation or evolution of our lives. That's the meaning of our brain, of our destiny, of being able to apply knowledge to change the world. We can help regulate our processes. We can create our lives.

Self Dialogues

The dying event is a special time in which we begin to resolve unendedness. Aspects of the person that have been unexpressed or unlived now can be free to express themselves. These many needs may not make themselves known in words or pictures. The dying event may be marked as an experience in sensations, moods, feelings, pulsation, vibrations and other perceptions not part of one's mundane awareness.

It could be said that long, lingering dying tends to occur in people who refuse to let some aspects of themselves find expression or who try to insist that one aspect or a small number of aspects maintain the upper hand at all costs. Or it could be that the person experiences the dying event pleasurably, and is attempting to extend it. It could be said that the length of one's dying event is related to the speed of inner resolution among all the unexpressed aspects of himself. And it could be posited that pain in dying results from resistance toward one aspect's attempt at expression.

I wonder if one can die only when all of the self is in harmony about dying. Or the opposite possibility: one dies suddenly as an expression of distress from one unheeded or ignored aspect to the others. In either case, I assume one can gain access to the template of his dying program to the extent that he can establish and maintain contact with non-verbal aspects of himself and let those aspects have expression in his life.

Self dialogues give the many sides of the self a chance to express themselves. Self dialoguing encourages the social aspect to surrender its position of domination up to other aspects. The self dialogue gives value to the what or how of our endings, a way to the unlived or unevoked; it makes senselessness obsolete, a way for revealing one's programs, a way of reading one's secret messages and a way that the dying person can derive meaning and purpose in their dying.

Self dialogues are simply how we talk to ourselves about ourselves, and how this talking is expressed through memories, feelings, sensations, images and character roles. Self dialogues are also how we make our mythology, how we teach ourselves, how we maintain or break up our boundaries, how we maintain or break up our sense of continuity, and how we discover and incorporate or deny the unexpected. Self dialogues are patterns, programs and scripts which feel right to us, determine our uniqueness and form our judgments. These patterns fall into two categories: there are social programs, which include rules about contact with ourselves and with others, how we have been taught to behave and the roles we are taught to play; there are biological programs, which include all those behavior patterns that have been given to or built into the organism — breathing, eating, digestion and elimination, sleep, sexuality, birth, dying and the functions of the autonomous nervous system.

Most people find themselves in their dying situation unexpectedly because they have avoided making contact with, or didn't know how to sustain or develop connectedness to their biological scripts. For instance, the visceral aspect may have been telling the neural aspect, "I'm ready to die now," or the neural aspect may have been frightened because it's afraid for its life, or it may have ignored the visceral aspect so long it didn't recognize it. And now the person is in the hospital with a very debilitated body wondering what's going on and believing that death has cut them down suddenly and unmercifully. And of course this attitude is reinforced by the family and by the doctors, since none of these people can be really aware of what's been going on in the dying person's myth. In this sense, the dying person's debilitated body is just the tip of their own iceberg.

Or it may be that the brain started to tell the social self, "You're going to die so tell the stomach to start dying," like the person holding a gun to their own head. And then one of the aspects, the brain or the visceral, got very freaky and said, "I'm not ready." Dying can be as a signal from one aspect of the self to another. When some of the aspects are not on speaking terms, one aspect may get very anxious about it while another does not.

Most people try to solve their problems by thinking things through, by imagining alternatives or by putting themselves in another person's shoes. This is one way to attempt a self dialogue, but it can leave one dissatisfied. It usually means that one side of us gets its way by effectively shutting off our needs or the protests of other inner aspects — either by judging, by being reasonable, or by self-intimidation. A solution is reached but one remains slightly dissatisfied because the stifled aspect did not get the chance to answer back or to defend itself.

Developing a self dialogue is learning how to arrive at solutions by letting every aspect have its say, so that the solution is a true resolution of one's deeper scripts. To identify all the inner characters, see what each has to say, what are their differences and whether there can be a conversation among them is to create a new synthesis in one's self-understanding and new possibilities for life expression.

I think of my self as being governed by a board of directors, without a permanent chairman. All the identifiable characters of my self have a seat, and new characters are always welcome. Looking around my board, I see the arguer, the reasoner, the sensible one, the justifier, the punisher, the lover, the religious one, the mother, and the father. In one day I might play a few or all of these roles, or more.

I also identify my feelings, which communicate through emotion, and my sensations, which communicate at any point in my body through temperature changes, small motions, pressure changes, weight changes, etc. Then I can identify my images which are expressed through pictures and visions, and my dreams which communicate with words, pictures, feelings, sensations and memories when I sleep. There is also my memory, that uses words, pictures, feelings and sensations to recall social and personal events. Then there is my biological director, which controls all involuntary body functioning and which defines my physical boundaries in the world, and that communicates with patterns of movement and with my imitation or adoption of other people's voices and gestures. I also count my sexual part, the urge to reproduction and to orgasm, and my universal aspect, that part of me connected with all the people who have ever lived or now live and with the life force, and which can find expression through the wisdom of the genetic code and through the manifestation of guides at the deepest levels of my being.

These are the regular members, but as I want to emphasize, there are plenty of chairs around for new members or unusual members who may show up in unusual circumstances, who may appear only once, or whose appearance may signal a whole new cycle of events. Also, this cast of characters is not intended to be definitive; it is in fact purposefully sketchy in order not to categorize or restrict experience, only stimulate it. Notice that only the first two of these board members communicate with words. That means that most of the aspects of myself are non-verbal. I function mostly outside the framework of mundane activity our society delineates as the hallmark of livelihood.

In other words, my organism has a logic of its own, an intelligence of its own, a mode of reasoning based on awareness. The affirmation of my life as process is expressed through all the members of my board when I identify with them all. It is the unfolding of their interaction that I call my mythology. Just as sometimes one member will be chairman of the board and sometimes another, so sometimes I will feel identified with my ego aspect or with a certain social role — such as the father — and other times I will feel identified with my feeling aspect or my dreaming aspect or my sexual aspect.

For the dying person, living their myth means realizing that *they are their own death,* they have chosen it, and that they are more than "consciousness," or body, or social roles, which must be ended in dying.

The ego aspect says "I" and thereby lays claim to the entire organism. The social aspect supports the ego's claim. These two verbal aspects try to overrule the rest of the board members and deny organismic process. Such is the nature of socialization that it interrupts and overrides the regular functioning of one's inner scripts. But this functioning is the ritual of the organism's existence. Simple examples are: going to sleep at night and getting up in the morning, breathing in and breathing out, getting hungry and feeling nourished, getting fatigued and becoming rested, getting sexually excited then releasing into orgasm. When one begins to let these events impinge on himself, process begins to alter social programming.

Process reveals itself by the events of your life, some of which are ritualistic and recurring, some of which are not — called spontaneous. Increasing experience of process moves your attention away from the ego and the social aspect. You begin to discriminate the life of your body from the roles of the society.

For example, fatigue is a message to rest from the visceral aspect that breaks into your awareness when your social self is holding your attention. At the time you may be in the middle of a spirited conversation, or concentrating on some part of your job, or driving through traffic. Fatigue is a strong message which, if ignored, leads to illness.

The fatigue message first begins as a dialogue between the visceral self and the social self. It grows from the social self ignoring or disregarding or overriding this dialogue. Fatigue is therefore a door to a part of one's self which you may enter by concentrating on your feelings.

The society calls business, scientific and other established social roles normal life. This may make you believe that what does not fit this scheme is crazy, bad or frightening. But this judgment is made only by the introjected social critic. This judgment is one of the dominators or tyrannicalizers of our board meetings. To know this is to begin to alter social conditioning.

Each board member is a euphemism for many complex processes. Just as your ego or social self expresses itself in a myriad of ways, so too the feeling self has a wide spectrum of feelings and memories. In fact, each board member has a natural range of feelings and actions. You may know your feeling aspect through sadness one day and anger the next. You may experience the dreamer in you through a nightmare. Or you may meet the action self through shoulder tension. Each of us has these many selves and more.

Developing Self Dialogues

Developing self dialogues does not mean analyzing yourself, criticizing yourself or problem solving; nor is it attempting to resolve conflicts. Process is the interaction of all of our living selves. The goal is experiencing ourselves in all our biological richness.

Aspects of the self do not exist in isolation, but in interaction. One does not experience a single aspect of self apart from others, but it's possible to experience their pattern of cooperation or non-cooperation.

I think of a client who told me he felt sad but didn't know why. I explained to him how he might make contact with whatever his sadness was connected to, which might reveal part of his script. After several weeks he told me his feeling of sadness reminded him of his girlfriend and of his mother. Months later, he commented that his feeling of sadness told him about the way he saw the world and the way he responded to it. He realized that he saw women as helpless, and responded with sadness. He found out through this experience something of his script about women, and about his sense of sadness.

Developing a self dialogue is a way to connect with aspects of experience that are unverbalized, unpictured and uncategorized. These aspects seem to be a direct knowing or experiencing. They are experiences we live but can't explain. Compared to a stage play, the introduction of each character into the body of the play could be the introduction of each unspoken desire, feeling and need. These characters' interactions are reflected on the stage of our imagination, our dreamlife and our experiences.

Developing self dialogues is holding a conversation with our board members, a conversation without words, a conversation in which silent or unknown parts of ourselves begin to speak.

Ego aspects show up as goals and self-recognition patterns. This is the part that always seems to create dualities, to measure things, to be compared to, to evaluate events as good or bad, and that creates or relinquishes boundaries. This aspect may show up in dreams in a consistent role, always doing the same activity or always the self behind the eyes that "see" the dream.

The social aspect is that part that internalizes and acts out social roles as though they were created from within. This aspect is concerned with "proper" behavior. Techniques of bioenergetics and gestalt therapy have successfully pointed out how one acts out the mother or the father, the protector and the punisher, the arguer, the martyr, the rebel and so on.

The dreamer in us is a direct conduit to the life of our deeper selves. Dreams are very complex and open to many possible interpretations. People who are patient enough to keep dream journals over a period of years begin to see patterns emerge from this rich terrain. At least one culture, the Senoi of the South Pacific, are famous for constructing their society around their dream life. The structure of Jungian therapy is systematic dream analysis and interpretation — a very intense process over a period of time. Look for patterns in your dreams. It helps to describe them regularly to a friend.

How do you fall asleep? How is falling asleep different from ordinary awareness? See how far down you can follow the process before sleep overtakes you. Notice your attitudes and sensations. Is there a pattern to going to sleep? Do you have a special ritual you use or a special space you enter? If so, see what you can find out about these habits without altering or evaluating them.

When you lie on the floor, then stand up, what keeps you from falling back to the floor? Your muscles and bones? Your "decision" to remain standing? As you stand, how many muscles in your body can you relax without falling? Many people prevent anxiety through muscular contractions. Patterns of these contractions relative to standing can be learned and even passed down from parent to child. These contractions are attitudes that form part of our personality. If you are aware or can become aware of a gesture or a facial expression you automatically make "just like Mom" or "the way Dad did it," you will have discovered one example of a silent self dialogue and will be learning how you create your body attitudes.

Western medicine has always assumed people could have no influence over involuntary or autonomic systems of the body such as heartbeat, temperature and blood pressure. Studies of stress and the development of bio-feedback training have recently changed that opinion. Studies of the breath by such people as

Alexander Lowen, Wilhelm Reich, and Karl-fried Durckhiem have tried to encourage the expression and emotion of the body.

By lying quietly, eyes closed, what quality of feeling comes from your breathing and your pulse? This will help you experience your body from inside toward the surface. Sensations, feelings and qualities of excitation will spread in a pattern to different parts of the body, giving rise to urges and images of action, letting us build the language of our story.

Connecting with ourselves in this way focuses us, giving a sharpened experience of ourselves and defining our mythology. As my friend Sam Bois, the semanticist, wrote me in response to reading a draft of this book: "In accepting new experience and formulating it to myself, I enter a new world that I have created out of which I emerge different."

Changing Perceptions

There is not just one way of being alive. Life, in the words of Bois, is multi-ordinal.* Life is experienced on many levels. Each level has its own unique range or spectrum of experience, its own validity. Each level has autonomy and cannot be dismissed or reinterpreted by another level.

When I say "go to sleep" and watch myself leave the awake world, I enter another, one with a different time and a different space. This dream world is not unreal. It is a particular kind of reality, different from ordinary reality.

It took a long time to learn the language of little dying. I had to differentiate between observing it and experiencing it. Our common system of knowledge is based upon the idea of distancing ourselves from an object in order to learn about it. We practice gaining knowledge through distance and observation. But we're part of an evolution toward a new subjectivity. We are

*The Art of Awareness, Wm. C. Brown Co., 1966.

moving, as a culture, further and further away from the old scientific, distanced way of making objects of the world. We are moving toward more participation in it.

Once I discovered that many of my fears of dying were related to programmed observations, I began to establish the connection that the socialized world teaches us to perceive living in a particular way. We are encouraged to agree, to act "as if" this is true. We then resist having this "civilized" world picture altered; we fear being crazy. We are unprepared for a life of changing experiences and perceptions. Any deviation is threatening. So we tend to dismiss unusual experiences, belittle and devalue the unusual as not being reliable, as not presenting a true picture. Few of us have been willing to be different.

Dying is entering another order of perceptions, a realm that is with us all the time, but is usually denied. Our sense of time, space, emotion and relationships must get altered. Dying can be exciting if you value moving toward the unknown.

Traveling in an auto, I was struck broadside by another one. I was thrown from the car. In a sudden moment everything became magnified; there was an incredible and indelible sense of detail. Time was a slow motioned focused close up, a panorama of vibrant color and sound. All ordinariness was gone. I was totally immersed in and aware of these immediate events which could have been my last moments of life. I was without fear, I was in wrap-around perception. I must say it was beautiful.

An old Gregory Peck/Alfred Hitchcock movie ends when Peck is shot down. We see him fall, then the camera shifts quickly to look out and up through his dying eyes. The circular stairway overhead, which he has just descended, begins to spin and fade. A spinning, falling, a shrinking, receding image, endeavors to capture this dimension of expression, to give an immediacy of what dying may be like not different from my experience in the auto accident.

Most people recognize their lives entirely in a world of symbols — words, thoughts, other verbal concepts. But everyone, whether they can recognize it or not, lives within a patina or pattern of sensations, images, fantasies and various configurations of feelings that are not verbal. Connecting with this non-verbal existence challenges our accepted, institutionalized, social world view.

We fear losing our known world to unfamiliar sensations and feelings. We hinder ourselves from being overwhelmed. Sometimes when friends tell me of a new experience, and of their fear of being overwhelmed by it, I ask them to tell me what is the place they are afraid of not being able to get back to? Where are they now that makes them think this is a place worth not losing? What is it like to be in transition between the known and the unknown?

When I am leading a group of people, someone usually will tell me that they feel nothing. I remind them that nothing is also an experience. What is this perception of nothing like — anesthesia? Let it speak. The experience of nothing, as well as any other unusual perception, can be a bridge, can be the very tool to more connection with the self. To feel nothing may be a statement of where we wish we were, or of what frightens us. From this nothing something can grow. These perceptions may or may not be what your dying will be like, but they may give you some hint of the unknown and how you accept or reject it.

Living your dying is being able to accept changing perceptions as a real part of self-experience. To accept an unusual experience without fear of judgment can mean going against the cultural model, but it allows us to affirm what is rather than what should be. Mountain climbers who have fallen hundreds of feet into snowbanks later related that their entire life flashed before them in great detail during the fall. Last year in California a 17 year-old skydiver jumped from a plane, then both of his chutes failed to open. He fell several thousand feet onto the asphalt runway, and survived with only a broken nose. He reported the same "hallucinatory" experience — his life flashing by as if in review.

A mathematician I worked with was lying down once when he suddenly appeared to stop breathing. He looked lifeless, as though in a trance. I called to him. Finally he roused himself. He told me he was enjoying quite a pleasurable wonderful feeling. He knew of my concern, was aware of me, but wanted the reverie he had uncovered. Thinking about this, I tried the following experiment. I imagined that the room was moving away, as though being at the end of a tunnel. Sounds seemed to travel over a great distance before reaching my ears. Noises seemed to echo and to spin me. The tunnel was a vortex distancing me from the world. I was shrinking, becoming smaller, spinning around and around like going down the drain of a bathtub. I sensed that the world was receding.

I got small, ten years old. Seven years. Then three years. Smaller still. I was a dot in space, a being unborn. There was a parade of light streaming through the darkness. Void. Then a flash; suddenly I expanded. Rapidly I grew bigger and bigger. Bigger than the room. Bigger than the house. Bigger than a block of houses.

Changing experiences are process — they either expand or explode the world, or shrink and break contact with it. Changing perceptions do not mean I am ill or insane. If I am losing my mind I will not have nothing when it is lost. But what I may be may not fit the cultural definition of normal or usual.

The culture tells us to hook our lives to memory and to projection. Thus we cling to the past or the future and compare it with the present. Experience tells me life is process. My changing, growing perceptions help separate out the society's mythology of dying and cultivate my own experience, my personal mythology.

Imagine a flow, or a stream, a jet of water, moving inside yourself, whether it starts in the belly or the head makes no difference. This flow of water or rain or sun or electricity moves through you as a stream of excitation, of excited light. As you imagine it moving, differentiate in your body between imagining it and experiencing it. "Ah, I imagine it, I see a picture, or whatever. I also feel it, I can localize it in me." Is there a separation of this imagination from you? Separate thinking about it from experiencing it. Can you separate out what is occurring from the pictures and the conceptions you have? Can you accept this type of experience?

If you will, be this flow of excitation now. What do you say to you? When I did I found my excitement to be of high intensity or low, sharp or dull. It came and went. It was all over me, resonating my head, my body. At this point I had no images, no thoughts, no conceptions. I was an ocean, a resonating pattern of excitation, a pulsating, a vibrating. This was my space where I was without boundaries. Perhaps dying, in a similar way, can be the willingness to be alive without any images or boundaries of what death might be.

The Desire to Die

The lust to live. We are born to want, we are born with the feeling of living, the wish to enjoy. The fevers we run, the violence with which we assert our needs, the fist we clench to endure, are testimony of our lust to live, to be open-ended.

My father told me, after he had undergone a surgery, that due to complications he almost died. In jest I replied ''Why didn't you?'' Astounded, he said: ''I was afraid. I like living. I love living.''

I have chosen to be born and I will choose to die. What a relief. The burden of my being a victim, hunted by death, vanishes. There are aspects of me that are willing to end at any moment and others that are not. I live out many endings in my life's story. The decision to die is made to avoid dying mechanically, routinely, just another death, not my end. I want an ending like my life, wherein I am not just carried by the stream of life like the current in a river. I think of the Kabbalistic teaching that a man has to learn to swim upstream against the current or he never knows who he is. The ability to say no, to inhibit the flow of excitation, the flow of life, guarantees individuality. The desire to die is the willingness to live my life and my dying. In this sense, my ending is a suicide.

This kind of thinking is taboo. This act is called self-murder. So I agree to let others kill me, or I pretend I let myself die. We all know more about dying than we care to or want to admit. The extreme of this attitude is that we kill ourselves voluntarily. Either the culture kills me or I end myself.

The desire to die is in everybody and comes up in everybody sooner or later. It springs from the organism with a lively thrust. It is a healthy passion, a natural passion, the same as sexual desire. It grows from within us, we inherit it. Our genetic code knows about dying; it knows how to end and even under what circumstances when to get started. The question of suicide comes down to: "Do I have to admit to myself that I want to die before I am a suicide?"

We limit the responsibility we are willing to take for our lives to a narrow range of decisions. Only actions committed in violation of these narrow bounds are culpable. We allow so-called natural dying but not self-dying. We admit we die, but not that we terminate ourselves. We can allow others to take our lives, but we prohibit ourselves from overtly ending ourselves.

A psychiatrist friend told me of a black woman with TB who lived in total poverty and despair in Georgia. Somehow she got in a very famous hospital for chest diseases in Colorado, where she made a very good recovery. However, the better she got the more anxious she became. The threat of going back to the life style of her past, and her inability to stay in Denver with no skills or money, was devastating for her. She kept saying, "Mabel is going to die," over and over. She died over a two week period. An autopsy showed there was no pathology to cause death. One could say Mabel died of despair. There were no alternatives she could live with, she could not be sick, she could not be well. She got the love and care she needed, but would not get it any more. She did not know how to get it. In this turning point, in the loss of her caring, her feelings of helplessness and her actual helplessness set up a state of hopelessness, that her brain must have recognized as a situation that called for death. She could not and did not extend herself. She chose a congealing dying. She was helpless. She accurately predicted her own death. She acted on her desire to die. She was not passive, she was a suicide, an active dier, ender.

The myth is that death is an enemy to be overcome, that it gets you sooner or later, and that it is intrinsically evil. Nowhere is violent death openly advocated as our preferred way to die. Persons who live out this mythology in their deaths receive such rewards as the culture can give. They died "bravely," "heroically," "after a long struggle," "meaningfully" and so on and they get bronze plaques.

In a culture that offers so many positive rewards for undergoing stress, such as social prominence, high salaries, fancy lifestyles and power, it can be argued that deaths from stress diseases (high blood pressure, certain kinds of heart disease and many rare diseases) are cultural deaths. Perhaps suicide, the desire to die, is condemned because it denies the twin myths of human productivity and cultural advancement. We need compulsive, achievement-oriented workers to maintain our social goals. The decision to die strikes at the very heart of this need. Persons who embrace the culture's values and succeed in their lives on its terms may be said to be living the culture's life. They may also have to live its death. The newspapers are full of examples.

The decision to live your own dying is the decision to reserve the right to end yourself. It is the decision to accept responsibility for your living and your dying. It is the decision to make contact with your living, your dying.

In other times and other cultures we find excellent precedent for taking one's life in one's hands. Quoting St. Thomas' *Summa Theologica:* "If you read in the Gospels it says 'Christ cried out in a loud voice and He bowed His head and He died'." St. Thomas was stating that Christ chose the moment of His death. He created His own death. He was not passive in the face of death. Death did not come to get Him. Christ defied the mythology that death comes to get you. Christ chose this martyrdom and He knew it. There are many statements in the Bible showing that Christ understood His dying style and lived it.

Christ gave Himself the command to free His spirit, to surrender His being, or whatever language He used. I give myself the command to disintegrate. I give myself the command to go to sleep and to die. To end.

In the past, Eskimos lived in a controlled environment, where their food supply was strictly limited. At a certain age everyone went out into

the snow to freeze. Here were a people who successfully condoned suicide without morbidity.

There are many examples of Buddhists
dying in meditation, examples that make it abun-
dantly clear that they chose the style of their
dying, and often times the time of their death as
well. Philip Kapleau, in *The Wheel of Death*,
recounts many stories of these voluntary
suicides.

It is my opinion that a person is ready to end,
or the dying process really gathers momentum,
when they feel that their experiences have reached a point where they can't expand, or can't be
assimilated as action in the world. We may be
ready to die because we have lived our lives out,
we have lived our existence. We have filled our
space, and now we remove ourselves from that
space.

The willingness to live my own dying is my
willingness to take the power over my death
away from the institutions: the doctors, the law-
yers, the morticians. It also means the
willingness to become aware of social dying programs that I am living, and avoiding or overriding them. And it means the willingness to
know that dying is me and that I have my own
dying program.

Suicide does not have to mean jumping from windows any more than it has to be voluntary. But suicide can be the ultimate affirmation of human freedom. It can also be a way of rejecting a death one is afraid of and a way of affirming choice. Suicide can be a deeply religious act.

Two people I knew who had lived together for a long time in a very creative relationship that had many mutual dependencies were suddenly faced with a terrible dilemma. The woman developed a serious debilitating illness the history of which was increasing pain and helplessness. She was then in her seventies. Facing her diminishing future squarely, she took it upon herself to straighten out her social affairs, in order that she could end her life with dignity. She hoped to avoid most of the culture's way of dying her kind of death, in a hospital all doped up. Instead she chose a way of ending which was to collect herself and avoid a lingering withdrawal from the world.

Her husband, a creative man in good health, decided he would rather die with his wife than survive her. He wished to maintain his bond with her. He did not want to bear the pain and loneliness of her loss and the difficulites of forming new relationships. He, too, chose his style of dying.

Together they quietly finished their social affairs, dressed and took sleeping pills. Their dying was a surprise to their friends and relatives, but they had planned it thoroughly and it occurred without morbidity. They could die as living — their dying was their living. Mabel died but never knew she could do her own dying, never knew she could find ways to be alive while dying. Participating and non-participating are the differences between the animal world and the human. Submission or participation. We can alter our circumstances; animals cannot.

There is one world and many. We live in one world. We can live in many. There is not one body, there are many. We do not die in one world but in many. The world(s) we live in is the world(s) we die in. I know at least four; each has a self, a body. There's a mechanical world of biochemical and anatomical structure. There's a vegetable world with its tree-like blood system and nervous system. There's an animal world, the emotional world. And there's the human world of created values and relationships. We live in all these worlds. The first three are given; the human one we enter and create. We all become human and more or less develop our humanness.

Each of these worlds has its own way of

dying with its own imagery, either determined or capable of being created. I'm saying that in the first three worlds death is a given, an inescapable predetermined event. In the machine world parts break down. Structure collapses. In the vegetable world cycles of growth lead to blossom and decay. In the animal world, the world of emotions and instinct, dying is either fearful or accepted. Animals die their fate, but they don't make it. In the human world we have the chance to make our fate, and to die it.

Reincarnation and a life hereafter seem to me to be a part of the vegetable world. But the question is not whether there is a life hereafter. The statement really is that we can choose to create and discover our own vision of the world and live it as we can, without dogma.

The brain mind operates by duplication, evidence and proof. In the realm of self-experiencing there is knowing without the need for proof. We have the choice to live either of these realms, or both. Taking our experience seriously in whatever realm it appears is living our life and its dying.

In waking and sleeping, the arena of volition is a thin line. I decide to go to sleep each night, but if I didn't, exhaustion would claim me anyway. I think of the childhood prayer: "Now I lay me down to sleep / I pray the Lord my soul to keep / And if I die before I wake / I pray the Lord my soul to take." Sleep is a drill, a voluntary surrender to the unknown. Sleep is a little dying, an ending.

The decision to integrate our dying style, to not fear dying as a viable alternative, strengthens our life. Life grows richer; not more morbid. Dying can be morbid for many people or a rationalized defeatism. This is resignation. The person who loves life, who participates in their dying, can risk living creatively and dying so.

The knowledge of dying is an expression of living, of healthy-mindedness, as we integrate and expand ourselves. Life is living, unaccountable varieties of living. The discovery that we end ourselves leaves the door open to living our lives and creating the known out of the unknown. Even death shaped by us.

Merging

Our dying gives our experience an intensity, an immediacy, a seriousness and an innocence that we have never known, or have forgotten. It's been my experience with people that the intensity and the vividness of the perception which is their life scares them. Most of the great mystics and saints talk about the exquisiteness of their experiencing and of their discovery, as Blake said, of the world in a grain of sand. Dying again returns us to this lingering of our senses, our emotions and events in the appreciation of the life we are in. Imagination cannot take us there; it can only prepare us for the event.

When we step out of our social roles, when we disengage ourselves from our programmed fears, when we immerse ourselves in the river of self-experiencing, we are bathed, merged in the non-verbal, non-conceptual, non-visual, non-idealistic world. We are indeed in the sea of creation. We are the sea from which we create our own lives. When you find your own answers, it is you.

The Center for Energetic Studies

The Center for Energetic Studies is a program of teaching, workshops and publishing under the direction of Stanley Keleman. Study at the Center focuses on the life of the body and the development of bodily process as the basis for living—how individuals form both themselves and their world.

Programs are led by Keleman and other leaders whose perspective is that the way we inhabit our bodies and express our emotions determines the human condition. Both laymen and professionals are students at the Center, participating in individual, group and extended learning programs.

The Center is located in Berkeley, California.

Published poet, painter, metal sculptor, author, group leader, educator, Stanley Keleman is renowned for his powerful charisma and gentle humanity. Born in Brooklyn, New York, he studied with Karlfried Durckheim at the Center for Religious Studies in Todtmoos, Germany. He was trained by Nina Bull, Director of Research for Motor Attitudes, Physicians' and Surgeons', Columbia University, New York and studied with Alexander Lowen, Institute of Bio-energetic Analysis, New York. He is senior trainer at both the Bio-energetic Institute, and the Gestalt Institute of San Diego, California. He is a workshop leader for Esalen Institute in San Francisco, works in Berkeley at the Center for Energetic Studies and conducts seminars and lectures all over the world.

Everyone wants to keep on living.
The way to keep on living is to
live your dying.